ISBN 978-88-6749-530-6 18 € / 20 $

9 788867 495306 >

and agglomerations,
of trees or

e agglomerati,
degli alberi o

To Laila, who brought me deep inside nature, beyond language

I would like to give back to this book some of the good it gave me and should give to many: namely, to feel the world differently, and to feel differently in a world the perception of which is transformed. How this transformation occurs is all the more difficult to describe as it involves means of extreme gentleness, far from any grandiloquence, from any presumption. This book takes us into the space and time in which we live and which we think we know, but at the same time it makes us feel that we really perceive them only in detached parts, that there is a gap, an infinite delay between what we know the universe to be made of in the abstract and what we make coexist in our perception and consciousness. "To hold therefore is to hold together," says one of these most beautiful texts—a call for a human ensemble to exist "above the void," its one and only foundation. But this also means learning to hold together the multiple operations of naming, identifying, classifying, and measuring, that weave the webs which wrest from the unknown that surrounds the human species, such as, for example, holding multiple sorts of mangoes named in all languages together with exoplanets which, for us, are still only letters and numbers. The more we desire the unknown, the greater the field of questions raised by the existence of other living beings. A certain tree will find the water it needs to grow more easily than a family of refugees doomed to the confinement of a camp. So we must remember to think of a tree "as unity/and as group of objects and events," and to ask what are "a living being's criteria for making decisions," whatever it may be. The graphic materiality of the writing serves as an additional vector of perceptual transformation. The curved verses bend a plant's volume onto the page, launch the dense jumble of names or the momentum of celestial orbits, inscribe the effort of a gesture, flip the gaze in a mirror... Inventive superpositions break with, but do not deny, the gravity of inclusive writing, endowing binaries with elegance and movement, respecting a hesitation between two possibilities of which we need not choose only one. Botany, animals, galaxies, working lives, displaced lives—innumerable are the lives of all kinds, such that truly considering them requires us

> [to hold] each other in the dark   [to seek] that point in the hand of another
> where a vein or a tendon are not just bodies
> but moving clusters
> human events   trees and seasons

An agglomeration under the sign of chance—a new, stunningly open representation of existence?

Judith Balso, May 2022

and agglomerations,
of trees

or

concretions and natural history

the darkness of sleep corresponds perhaps to the blackness of space
for a few hours outside one's condition as an individual
a little whitewashed wall traced a perimeter
around an empty garden   full actually but of dark earth
confides anyone to another   seated at the cafeteria table
at break time   then while I was letting myself reach a state
of animal danger   imminent and without definite contours
that same area filled up very quickly
with wild flowers mostly white and pale yellow
and of many different shapes and sizes
while the external part stayed out of focus
as if crumpled yet smooth

for a long time   answers the other   the external part
did not differentiate   so I subtracted it
from my perception   and since it wasn't entirely
other than me   I was unknowable even to myself
because I wasn't other than myself or inside myself
and the world wasn't   outside of me   but there are states
and conditions into which we're sometimes brought without knowing it
where something   a blackbird in the grass   a branch moved
by the current   saves us   even if it isn't a
salvation without consequences

going shopping in a cheaper supermarket
adds a third middle-aged person sitting opposite   still
with a surgical cap and gloves   her/his daughter/son out of work
her/his husband/wife always watching television   by accident
we took a path beside a few cottages under construction
after a few metres the song (or was it a speech?) of the birds
pushed our view of the surrounds out of focus
as if crumpled yet smooth   while from where we were
they were then only animal sounds   tresses of trees
leaves and flowers in motion   mineral aggregates
framed by the arch of a blackberry bush   some pheasants
were moving on the front lawn like concepts   like interstellar clouds

it's time   someone passing by interrupts them
to go back to work   she/he taps his/her index finger on the handless face
of his/her wristwatch   then he/she walks away   in the darkness of space
seasons and individuals revolve in sequence
shading into one another   on this as on other inclined planets

the vine differs from other vines in several traits
its mature stem is wrinkled (as if knurled) grey in colour
but the bark doesn't split like that of other vines
it always has tendrils only simple (never forked) thick and robust
and a marked tendency to form buds

the bunches are irregular and normally have from around 6-8 up to 40 grapes
the grapes are fairly big with a thick hard skin
which is not ingested at consumption
often some of the grapes mature separately from the others
and are removed individually from the bunch

the leaves are fairly small (15-18cm) they are never lobed
but instead round with a rough dentation very thick and shiny

the plant has fruit (grapes) black (reddish-blue) and bronze in colour
very rarely red
the diameter of the grapes (always spherical or only subtly ovular)
ranges from 13mm to 38mm
when mature the grapes come off with great ease

the abscission (removal) of the bunch is very difficult

the fruit's unexpected thud   the leaf's gentle descent
are forms of the flow's twisting   modes of manifestation among the many
that can occur even without presence
and when we won't be here   those same trajectories
will restore body to the body   oneness to the aggregate

looking for that brain-shaped pear among the leaves near the fence
it seemed possible to accept that things are in motion
and that certain mistakes will not be redeemed
if not by the simultaneous vision of a tree as unity
and as group   of objects and events

"passed from one hand to the other at the market stall
it was stirring in the bag   stretching out its neck
seeking the air with its head   and its wings were fluttering
I was trying to move aside the vegetables and potatoes
which my guest had bought at another stall
and dropped in the same bag as if it were already
a dish   because I knew how afraid it was
and how it needed to breathe   how it was still
holding on to life   for no other reason
than life itself   this knowledge
I now think   is an immediate awareness that
like every form of feeling   belongs to every living thing"

fig. 107 close-up photograph of ripe fruit of the grevia asiatica
tree whose leaves are alternately

petiolate
cordiform
rounded
pointed
with 5 nerves
partially lobed
tomentous underneath

the size of apple leaves
flowers three in number

pedunculated
axillary

hort. angl. g. pelosa
warm stove

the membranes may be prepared in the form of flat leaves
tubes capillaries and hollow fibres

the methods for preparing artificial membranes are
synthesis
precipitation from evaporation
thermal precipitation
stretching a polymeric film
extraction
electrochemical means (with the electrochemical process called etching)

you've got to wake up soon for water

I have seven children and not enough water to drink

we have to beg our neighbours to give us water to drink

every day at the well women fight for water

after preparation the membranes may be assembled in
plates or frames (with an arrangement analogous to the filter press)
spiral modules
hollow fibre modules
in tubes or fibres from 0.25÷2.5mm in diameter
assembled together to form the module
in rectilinear configuration or in a U
tubular modules
with tubes greater than 3mm in diameter
usually assembled in geometries with heat exchange and casing
artificial membranes are used with organic polymers
or with inorganic material

organic polymers polysulfone (PS) polyethersulfone (PES)
cellulose acetate (CA) polyamide (PA)
polyvinylidene fluoride (PVDF) polyacrylonitrile (PAN)

inorganic materials gamma aluminum alpha aluminum
borosilicate glass

gravitational solar tides are probably
the principal cause of Venus's slow
rotation but do not explain its retrograde motion

documentation of its eclipse times shows that the day
has gotten subtly longer during the last two millennia

since the beginning of the year the east of the country accepts
thousands of refugees fleeing from conflict zones

arriving with almost nothing they were led progressively
further from the border to the interior
where a place was allocated by the authorities

the camp extends several hundred metres
one can see some workers hammering a surface
as they prepare a shelter
some agents that verify the details of the new arrivals

this Tuesday afternoon the inhabitants of the
nearby villages came to the camp to meet
the new arrivals and to offer food and clothing

"que dieu veille sur nos femmes et enfants
que votre souffrance arrive à terme
que le malade guérisse
que celui qui a tout perdu
retrouve la prospérité
que celui qui est sans abri trouve un toit"

fig. 353 close-up photograph of the spherical inflorescences of a néré tree
this straight-trunked smooth-barked tree

can measure 25m high and is composed of pinnately compound leaves
its foliage *is deciduous* after 5 to 7 years
the *tree begins to bloom* that hangs in clusters
its fruit is a big pod covered in yellow pulp
containing *black* beans a tree can generate
called néré
up to 100 beans per year the fruit begins
to mature immediately after the first rains and continues
for the greater part of the season

the tree has a taproot able to seek water
at a depth of up to 60 metres

the tree is primarily pollinated by bats *bees*
flies wasps ants *and beetles*
it has been demonstrated that the foliage *of a néré*
contributes to the fertility of the soil

three fundamental questions

1 spores and the way they move and reproduce particularly
when photosynthesis is not possible

2 the behaviour and presence of apparently immaterial things
that spread through space

3 a living being's criteria for making decisions
for example how a plant that has flowers of several colours
decides to assign this or that colour to a certain flower
or why a bird perched on a branch
suddenly flies away even in the absence
of food of a predator or of its own kind to reunite with

even if the fog forms a membrane over the expanse   beyond the water
the swaying of the treetops can be shared
the grass invites us out   to partake under the snow
giving itself in the form of the possible
a plastic clock wrenched from its clasps flutters
beneath an overpass
partially obscuring a rest stop

maybe for once it's not about resisting the real
trying to climb back up time
I would like to tell you as I greet you   close the door
and go down the street   up to the void to fill it with wood and branches
maybe that film behind the mass of matter
was shot the day we'll all be together   at home
listening between star and lava   beyond the beginning
while a liquid formation comes down ceaselessly
in front of a streetlamp   onto the leaves
a passage of growth and not of degeneration
afternoon of space   dovetail of seasons
beneath the grass   out of the days
beyond the flood   after the fog
the trees   sway

what happens when I switch off
and the silence invades me from above?
not every truth is found in the delivery van
not every memory in the light that changes with an unexpected
movement of the clouds

if we turn into the wind glowing between the branches   the voids between things
go away   we'll be able to search for an extension
or the fruit's rough surface   and to accept
that something at times at signs may die

just inside the wood   the sun is out of sight
in the growing darkness shines a mass of objects
white in winter   green in summer
the step crunches on this organic film
made of layers and paths   streetlamps and concepts
if you say for example that we are not alone you have to lower the rope down
into the hole that unites us   find food
to accept the void and recognise it behind the screen
against fear   a vertical vertigo
a body seeking
animal language
mass of objects expanding horizontally   green in winter
white in summer   tree and antenna at dusk
from where to call   from where

"after a hard night"
"yes"
"the gaze rests on nearby objects and smoke from an outside chimney"
"that silently filters a mountain and its houses"
a surface of sun projected from the window unreels
a different narrative   a rope around the neck
does not hinder an animal from turning and sensing the air
the sloping firs   the story of grass
the clouds smooth the vertical view   and give it back to the forest

I saw you inside the wood turning childhood over
finding the air in the pillow
and sinking again into space
the firs and the pines like an orchestra   like the others together
listening to the seasons

the glass covers only a portion of day
fear only a portion of night   snow
only a portion of voice

the peak's curved lines   lake and moon   lake to moon
and the firs above in darkness give roots to the next morning
daylight slanting like the peak's curved lines
lake and light   lake to light   the trunk spins and thickens
clay beneath grass beneath snow beneath the bounce of a bird
or the step of an animal slowly starting down a slope that
slants like the day's fall

beneath the trees in the roots of the next night
an animal breathes   moves in space
forever altering the distribution of grass and earth
before the total night   earth and darkness
earth to light in every declivity of space
along the lines of the peak where the grass and the cliff are active even when
no one passes   even when unobserved
the stone determines the curve of perception
and traces a web of events
roots and rock   rock to roots
to   and

and agglomerations of trees

o r

⊙

⊙

⊕

in physics a black body is an ideal object
that absorbs all incident electromagnetic radiation
without reflecting it and is thus called black
according to the classic interpretation *of the colour of bodies*

Tesserae

it all started with this need to cut matter sitting in the city's worst bar to test joy's resistance in front of the pinball machines the slot machines the sticky tables and the news of the exodus of thousands of people and animals from some other city the HD photos of their suffering faces seem like something from a documentary or a movie the real concealed beneath information beneath the record of reality and yet it is a matter of holding of staying of holding tight that object in the grass and also of knowing how to let it go but what is our task how can we act without destroying ourselves how can we open the reality behind the fear it is certain that my task is not to tell my life as if it were more interesting than others even if many seem to prefer this path which is not a path only an illusion of control some patches of snow are left despite the temperature despite the voices that trouble the train's even noise these electric frequencies that show a continuity between our world and that of perception beneath the landscape and the void between the two panes and there's a substantial difference between the black lava rock placed on the chest and the rock forming in the chest because of the others of cutting matter of the voices that cover the even hum of the motor and the ringing of the machines in the grass through the trees beneath the slope where are we calling from where from where

and it's too dull to do as so many did to reject the feelings to limit oneself or to leave off at a description or to pretend that the simultaneous events of a city are sufficient to justify the existence of a form of representation it's true that we trace a line through the streets or beneath the hills it's true that one trajectory cannot be another and maybe that's precisely what hurts but how to feel or be without choosing these architectures without this even hum of insect wings or of the motor in the air every body endowed with movement or with the capacity for growth but also a stone or a machine moved by the current are subject to one direction not another and if we could record all their paths with a line of light the structure of motion would form a clot a mass of matter to cut anew in order to exist life as cause and end of this obliqueness swelling or dilation

left if I say Sophie left I trace a line over the line and reducing the possible to its representation is something truly different from being able to choose to accept the trajectory being able to fall in a bedroom backwards into mine and into your infant head and in the head of everyone who asks to listen in a bedroom backwards that is all the possible bedrooms all the spaces between the trees and in the oblique exits and in the cutting of matter Sophie isn't there Sophie is my daughter who doesn't exist yet and is therefore every possible daughter the world's whole daughter who sits at a table and spills out of a besieged city and therefore Sophie is not a character look at her features in this picture which isn't shown because it's not showable let's touch her billowing hair whose fibres contain the paths that she will run through the grass and through the buildings and with her I will try to retrace what I wasn't given knowing that the structure of motion that the spaces between the trees that the backwards bedroom isn't the same inclination in the cutting of matter and that we are not able to choose our own birth but we can instead choose to be born and to fall

Sophie took her keys and her bag and left the house on the landing she felt as if someone had dragged her out the door as if she hadn't crossed the threshold on her own Mrs. Maxwell was as usual passing a wet rag over the faux marble stairs they greeted one another politely and with a faint and indefinite suspicion

here Sophie is not my not-yet-conceived daughter but a woman who exists inside me and whom I share parts of my story with but not this story Sophie came down the stairs and snuck into the subway line 2 or 6 is not line 1 or 5 and it's not like tracing a space between the trees Sophie was feeling inside and outside inside the car between the dull gazes of a couple of adolescents and those full of open voids of an old man and his dog and outside space because she was tracing a trajectory through a movement that however did not depend on her she started walking against the train's motion then she said to herself that there wasn't a reason always to resist the real

in that moment Sophie like all of us wasn't only a face and a body not only a movement and a clot of thoughts and sensations she was also everything that she had been before her whole actual existence as a young woman of whom even if we had more details we wouldn't know anything because to know something it's necessary to remember that we are stones corpuscular constructions and neurological stratifications nonverbal animal Sophie's whole being vibrating in the subway Sophie naked beneath the clothes she'd put on that day a bit randomly randomly that day Sophie who with an arbitrary choice could now stay on the subway forever continue on until we think of her movement through space as caused by an electric motor that emits a constant buzz on which is superimposed every now and then the low voice of an old man sitting across from her who says something to his dog it's unclear if he's scolding it or if his are words of love for that stellar magma for that animal body that weave of tissues to which everyone belongs Sophie included if we decide that they are not characters

these pictures says Sophie's mother while Sophie isn't there because her trajectory in the subway continues indefinitely and indiscernibly these pictures says Sophie's mum as she shows them to an interlocutor without eyes or form these pictures were taken that summer when we will all be together at home when Sophie will have left the subway when the dull gazes will have become rocks shiny from the undertow beaten by the movement of the sea that summer when we will be all together and there will be no more conflicts or divisions or hierarchies Sophie's mother and Mrs. Maxwell are two immeasurable bodies in this temporality two formless bodies like the interlocutor's united as stellar mass as animal tissue outside the glass door far from the intercom and the stairs always more liquid always more permeable by air and by the configurations of external atoms like the sea like the undertow into which little Sophie runs laughing against the waves that are still unreeling backwards in the bedroom that Sophie's mum prepared at the exit from the subway

Sophie imagines that the man could be booted from the car before they arrive at the next stop but what is the next stop what is a stop what is the balance to be found between resisting the real and entering its flow where do we have to strike Sophie thinks with her whole body Sophie naked beneath her clothes inside her brain behind her eyes where can we strike and when instead can we stretch out on the grass in the undertow at home now that Sophie has left that she felt as if someone had dragged her out the door and down the stairs but away from which house

Sophie was feeling inside and outside inside and outside of Mrs. Maxwell whom she just encountered inside and outside her mother she hadn't seen for a couple millennia Sophie was tracing a line a vector in the city but without direction without temporality because Sophie is a set made of moving categories is the movement of the undertow that embraces and polishes the rocks is the cradle we all come from and on account of that the memory of something that hasn't yet occurred and of a past event past without name

Sophie doesn't have a name and Mrs. Maxwell doesn't have a surname Sophie's mum could have a name but doesn't as long as it isn't written and if it were written she wouldn't have it anymore we are located within indefinite objects that haven't yet occurred lines of the possible through eyes still closed this morning while you hold me in bed and murmur a message of beginning

Sophie doesn't speak any language that can be understood she breathes hard
smiles like a little girl like an animal

take her to buy some balloons in the park

is

and

tesserae

Inventory of all extant species of mango and the names and characteristics of several recently discovered exoplanets

B74
brooks
haden
irwin
keitt
kensington pride
kent
nam doc mai
palmer
R2E2
ashini
fazli
himsagar
khirshapat
langra
lokhon-bhog
raj-bhog
aug din
ma chit su
sein ta lone
shwe hin tha
coquinho
haden
manga espada
manga rosa
palmer
tommy atkins
cambodiana
ameliorée du
mango blanco
amelie
black (blackie)
bombay
dou-douce
east indian
graham
haden
julie (st. julian)
long
madame francis
rose
spice-box
starch
baiyu
guixiang
huangpi
huangyu
macheco
sannian
yuexi
haden
irwin
keitt
mora
tommy atkins
ambassador
alfonso
ataulfo
criollos
haden
julie
keitt
kent
reina
tommy atkins
alfonso
hindi
hindi besennara
beid el agl
oweisi
fuss oweis
taymoor
zebdiah
apple
carabaoo
kinalabaw
indian
piko
paho
pahohutan
haden
kent
tommy atkins
francine (madame francis)
muscas
labiche
baptiste
rosalie
poirier
corne
lil
ghausa
dusehri
gaddamar
ottu mangai
mulgoba
langra benarsi
khahpasand
badsha
surkha
rolapuri
fajli
himsan nara
alphonso
amrapali
badami

		0.86	10.57415		0.0143	0	79
		1.205	0.7668944	—	0.049	1.18	89
			0.014	—	0.032	0.0007	—
			3.778873		0.199	89.68	
						89.35	
						85.37	
TOI-1406 b	46	1.234	2.178	0.1436	—	—	—
NGTS-10 b	2.162	0.107	18.71204	0.231	0.11	0	86.8
OGLE-2017-BLG-1434L b	0.725	0.867	55.086	0.0681	0.01598	88.5	—
WASP-143 b	0.0085	0.3551	4.401131	0.141	0.31	88.5	—
HD 158259 b	0.244	1.642	24.45		0.31		
2020 HD 332231 b	0.12406	—	0.76552398	0.063	0.04394	0.22	87.98
HD 95338 b	21	0.30752	20.902	0.063	0.07098	0.047	87.43
KELT-25 b	—	1.57	20.902		0.01782	0	77.18
HD 79211 b	0.12831	1.57	4.066499		0.0318	0	82.01
TOI-849 b	39.3	0.3256	8.350381		0.03524	0	80.98
TOI-1510A b	40	1.5	0.9809734				
2020 A a	—	2.03	2.0845435				
2020 b	0.974	1.286	2.2554477				
TOI-1130 c	3.213	1.086	3.81433	0.0404	0	88.125	—
HIP 65A b	1.18	0.09707	0.01246	—	—	0.63	—
TOI-157 b	0.791				12.2	—	—
TOI-169 b	0.0132				162	—	—
HIP 1815 b							
OGLE-2018-BLG-0677L b							
OGLE-2019-BLG-1339/OGLE-2019/BLG-1019 b	—	14	3	—	0.012	0.064	85.9
KMT-2019-BLG-... b		0.11883	0.7683881		0.077	0.115	89.08
TYC 8998-760-1 b	0.00982	0.205	12.252048		0.04269	0.088	87.08
LTT 3780 b	0.0267	1.117	3.9228038		0.03769	0.162	89.58
LTT 3780 c	0.369	0.8	3.1316666		0.04515	0.071	88.27
HATS-47 b	0.243	0.765	4.1480467		0.066517		0.013
HATS-48A b	0.353	0.7224	7.3279474				
HATS-49 b	0.1254						
HATS-72 b	88.56						
KELT-2019-BLG-1953 c		0.28	—	—	0.8	—	—
KELT-2019-BLG-1953 b		0.59	—	—	0.8	—	—
2MASS J1155-7919 b		10	—	—	582	—	—
HD 191939 b	—	0.3007	8.880411		0.089	—	88.66
HD 191939 c	—	0.2873	28.5806	0.178	—	89.14	—
HD 191939 d	—	0.2819	38.3561	0.216	—	89.49	—
EPIC 249893012 c		0.04616	0.3274	15.624	0.13	0.07	87.94
EPIC 249893012 d		0.03203	0.3515	35.747	0.22	0.15	—
EPIC 249893012 b	0.0145	0.02753	0.174	3.5951	0.047	0.06	86.14
L 168-9 b	0.134	0.124	1.4015	0.02091	0.21	85.5	—
TOI-257 b	—	0.626	18.38827		0.1523	0.24	88.78
TOI-1338	—	1.606	71.4	—	—	—	—
2020 d	—	—	106.341	0.31	0.16	—	—
2020 A c	—	—	122.005	0.339	0.29	—	—
2020 b	0.0249	—	11.949	0.079	0.26	—	—
2020 d	0.00406	0.2346	36.052	0.178	0.03	—	—
TOI-700 c	0.00711	0.0901	16.051998		0.0925	—	—
TOI-700 d	—	0.1062	9.97701	0.0637	0.032	0.033	88.9
HD 158259 c	—	—	37.4326	0.163	0.032	89.67	—
HD 158259 d	1.41	—	3.432037	—	—	89.73	—
HD 158259 f	0.82	1.94	5.198	—	—	—	—
HD 158259 e	0.02357	0.1954	12.03	—	—	—	—
WASP-178 b	—	0.21751	7.954	—	—	—	—
Kepler-65 e			3.3448285	—	0.0558	—	—
K2-146 c			258.8	0.034	0.28	0	85.7
K2-198 d			4.00498		0.075	127	—
			7.4500177		0.05234	87.54	—
						—	89.86

(ma... ncis)

bangalora
banganapalli
bombay
bombay green
cheruku rasalu
chinna rasalu
pedda rasalu
fooman
fajri kalan
fernandian
gulabkhas
himayath
himsagar
imam pasand
jehangir
kalami
kesar
kishen bhog
komanga
lalbaug
langra
mallika
malgis
mankur
mankurad
moovandan
nattuma
neelum
pairi
priyor
rajapuri
raspuri
ratna
safeda
sammar bahisht
suvarnarekha
totapuri
vanraj
zardalu
alampur baneshan
arumanis
gadung
golek
manalagi
haden
keitt
kent
maya
nimrod
palmer
tommy atkins
kensington pride
glenn
tommy atkins
keitt
maya
van dyke
osteen
kent
patwi
boubo
ngowe
apple mango
apple rumani
arumanis
golek
kuala selangor
malgoa
maha-65
tok boon
amelie
kent
ataulfo
haden
irwin
kent
manila
palmer
sensation
tommy atkins
van dyke
petakon
oro
criollo
nino
chausa
dusehri
langra
desi
anwar rataul
sindhri
fajri
saroli
bagan pali
alphonso
muhammad wola
neelum
criollos
haden
keitt
kent
tommy atkins
carotte
jose

K2-198 c
K2-198 b
K2-168 c
K2-168 b
2019
K2-43 c
K2-33 b
EPIC 221416 b
HD
WASP-126 c
WASP-18 c
2019
WASP-18 c
2019
K2-291-18 c
TOI-263 b
PSR J2055+3829 b
2019
CWISEP J1935-1546
HAT-P-70 b
HAT-P-69 b
TOI-125 c
2019
TOI-125 d
TOI-125 b
2019
Borisov
2019
HD 1724 b
Kepler-1661 (AB) b
2019
HD 38677 b
2019
HD 1231 b
2019
HD 42936 b
2019
HD 38677 e
2019
HD 38677 c
2019
HD 38677 d
2019
HD 80653 b
TOI-564 b
TOI-905 b
XO-7 b
2019
OGLE-2013-BLG-0911L b
2019
EPIC 211939692.02
EPIC 211939692.01
2019
USco 1621A b
USco 1556A b
KMT-2019-BLG-0842 b
HIP 36985 b
2019
WD J0914+1914 b
2019
Kepler-154 g
GJ 40 b
OGLE-2016-BLG-1227 b
HIP 41378 g
beta Pic c
AB Dor C b
TOI-677 b
WISE 2150A b
HD 85628 A b
NGTS-8 b
TOI-132 b
OGLE-2015-BLG-1771L b
Proxima Centauri
WASP-185 b
WASP-184 b

—
—
—
—
0.2159
0.4024
0.1904
0.202
0.1737
—
—
—
6.78
3.58
0.02086
0.0428
0.0299
—
50.5
—
—
—
—
—
—
—
0.0176
1.463
0.667
0.709
1.373
2019
15
14
—
—
0.016
9.37
13
1.236
34
3.1
2.9
2.83
0.07183
0.98
0.57

0.12695
0.37372
0.11687
0.1659
2.198884
3.471149
0.836
—
—
0.2061
0.83
39
11
1.87
1.676
0.24614
0.2614
0.2432
0.000062
—
0.053
—
—
—
—
—
—
0.1439
1.02
1.171
2.8641424
—
—
—
—
10.28
—
—
0.9145
0.18066
—
—
—
1.179
—
1.53
1.09
1.07
0.306
—
1.25
1.33

3.3596055
17.0428683
8.050722
15.8523
0.0201
14.2767
7.63
2.1558
4.989963
0.556814
—
2019
—
2.74432452
4.7869491
9.15059
19.98
4.65382
44926
—
18.57
5.2049
6.6732
5.516
6.584
2.882
0.719573
1.651144
3.739494
10.08
0.232
0.232
—
—
—
8500
—
1250
5.746007
0.79
62.06
1238
—
11.2366
—
2.82406
2.1997
4.43527
2.1097008
0.433
—
9.38755
5.1817

0.0979
0.0148
—
0.1228
—
—
0.12959037293
—
0.0814
0.137
0.05186
—
26.3
175.06
0.1462
0.0664
0.0662
0.0651
0.0733
0.0422
0.02734
0.04421
—
39.553
26.8549
2880
3500
—
7
—
—
—
0.3227
2.72
0.58
0.1038
341
0.047
0.035
0.058
—
1894
0.0904
0.0627

0.03077
0.09083
0.06231
—
—
89.6
0.115
0.025
0.009
0.029392
0.01
—
0.04739
0.06555
0.066
0.168
0.194
—
0.63
—
0.083
0.083
0.14
0.07
0.057
0.07
0.0166
0.072
0.04666
0.038
—
—
—
—
—
3.31
0.55
0.07
0.15
0.0385
—
0.06
0.248
—
0.435
—
0
0.01
0.06
0.026
—
1.48
0.24
0

—
—
89.81
—
89.26
—
85.75
—
—
—
—
—
0
0
88.54
88.795
88.92
3.155
58.6
0.06
—
—
—
—
—
—
—
78.38
0.024
83.45
10.8
0.06
0.16
—
—
—
—
—
—
—
0
3.4
—
97.86
—
87.63
—
86.7
86.9
84.1
0.087
0.85
0
86.8
86.9

86.494
88.904
—
—
—
2019
—
—
—
—
86.96
—
96.5
87.19
—
—
—
—
—
89.464
—
—
—
—
—
—
—
82.1
85.68
—
—
—
—
—
—
—
—
—
—
—
88.57
—
—
—
84.63
—
—

86.494
88.904
lucie 0.03077 —
auguste 0.09083 — —
apple mango 3.3596055 0.06231 89.81 —
arumanis 0.12695 17.0428683 — —
golek 0.37372 8.050722 0.0979 — 89.26 —
kaem yao — 0.11687 15.8523 0.0148 — 2019
mangga dadol — 0.1659 89.6 85.75 —
alampur baneshan K2-198 c — 2.198884 0.0201 0.1228 0.115 — —
alice K2-198 b 0.2159 3.471149 14.2767 0.025 — —
alphonso K2-168 c 0.4024 0.836 7.63 — 0.009 — —
anderson K2-168 b 0.1904 — 2.1558 — 0.029392 —
angie K2-43 c — 0.202 — 4.989963 0.01 — 86.96
bailey's marvel K2-43 b 0.1737 0.2061 0.556814 —
bennet alphonso K2-221416 b — 0.83 0.12959037293 —
beverly 2019 — 39 2019 — — — —
bombay NA — 11
brahm kai meu NA
brooks 2019 SP-126 c
carabao 2019 SP-18 c
carrie 2019 291-18 c
chok anon LP 55 b
cogshall TOI-263 b 2.74432452 0.04739 0 96.5
cushman PSR J2055+3829 b 1.87 4.7869491 0.06555 0 87.19
dot 0.0001 J1935-1546 6.78 1.676 9.15059 0.0814 0.066 88.54 —
duncan CWISEP 3.58 0.24614 19.98 0.137 0.168 88.795 —
earlygold HAT-P-70 b 0.02086 0.2614 4.65382 0.05186 0.194 88.92 —
east indian HAT-P-69 b 0.0428 0.2432 — — 3.155 —
edward TOI-125 c 0.0299 0.000062 26.3 0.63 58.6 —
eldon 2019 TOI-125 d — — 44926 175.06 — 0.06 89.464
emerald 2019 TOI-125 b 50.5 0.053 — 0.1462 0.083 — —
fairchild 2019 2I/Borisov
fascell HD 13724 b
florigon 2019 Kepler-1661 (AB) b 2019
ford
gary
gaylour
glenn
gold nugget
golden lippens
graham
haden 18.57 0.1462 0.083 — —
hatcher — — 5.2049 0.0664 0.083 — —
ice cream HD 38677 b 2019 — — 6.6732 0.0662 0.14 — —
irwin HD 11231 b 2019 — — 5.516 0.0651 0.07 — —
ivory HD 42936 b 2019 — — 6.584 0.0733 0.057 — —
jakarta HD 38677 e 2019 — — 2.882 0.0422 0.07 — —
jean ellen HD 38677 c 2019 0.0176 0.1439 0.719573 0.0166 — 82.1
julie HD 38677 d 2019 1.463 1.02 1.651144 0.02734 0.072 78.38
keitt HD 80653 b 0.667 1.171 3.739494 0.04666 0.024 85.68
kensington pride TOI-564 b 1.373 2.8641424 0.04421 0.038 83.45 —
kent TOI-905 b 2019 10.08 — — 10.8 —
lancetilla XO-7 b 0.709 — 0.232 39.553 — 0.06 —
langra benarsi OGLE-2013-BLG-0911L b — 0.232 26.8549 — 0.16 —
lippens EPIC 211939692.02 15 — — 2880 — — —
mallika EPIC 211939692.01 14 — — 3500 — — —
manilita USco 1621A b 2019 — 10.28 — — 3.31 — —
mendoza USco 1556A b 2019 — 8500 7 0.55 — —
mulgoba KMT-2019-BLG-0842 b — — — 0.07 — —
nam doc mai HIP 36985 b 2019 0.016 0.9145 1250 — 0.15 — —
nam tam teen WD J0914+1914 b 0.18066 5.746007 — 0.0385 0 88.57
neelum Kepler-154 g 2019 9.37 — 0.79 — 3.4 —
nu wun chan G 9-40 b 13 — 62.06 0.3227 0.06 — —
okrung OGLE-2016-BLG-1227 b 1.236 — 1238 2.72 0.248 97.86
osteen HIP 41378 g 34 1.179 — 0.58 — —
palmer beta Pic c 3.1 — 11.2366 0.1038 0.435 87.63
parvin AB Dor C b 2.83 1.53 — 341 — —
pascual TOI-677 b 2.9 1.09 2.82406 0.047 0 86.7
philippine WISE 2150A b 0.07183 1.07 2.4997 0.037 0.01 86.9
pickering HD 85628 A b 0.306 4.43527 0.058 0.06 84.1
po pyu kalay NGTS-8 b 2.1097008 —
rosigold TOI-132 b 0.98 — 0.433 — 0.026 0.087 84.63
ruby OGLE-2015-BLG-1771L b 0.57 1.25 — 1894 — 0.85 —
rutledge Proxima Centauri 1.33 9.38755 0.0904 1.48 0 —
saigon WASP-185 b 5.1817 0.0627 0.24 86.8
sensation WASP-184 b 0 86.9
sophie fry
southern blush
spirit of '76
springfels
sunset
suwon tip
tebow
toledo
tom dang
tommy atkins
torbert
turpentine
valencia pride
van dyke
zill
hawaiian common
gouveia
hawaiian dwarf
kurahige
mapulehu
momi k
pope
rapoza
sugai
turpentine
fascell
haden
keitt
kent
sensation

— 1.083
0.0876 —
14.446 — —
— 0.019636 0.217 0.16 —
tommy atkins — 41.516 0.099 0.2 — —
zill 2019 15.144 0.063 0.2 2.15 —
alfonso — 7.76 — — — —
bez el-anza
oweisi
taymoor
dampara 2019 J2116+0234 b
hingurakgoda LSPM 2019 — — 0.0267 0.0857 0.0034 85.5
karutha colomban OGLE-2018-BLG-0532 b — — 0.0009 0.048 0.3 86.23
malwana amba HIP 35173 b — 3.58599 0.074 0.19 87.43
parrot mango HIP 54373 c — 0.18601 5.97293 0.1027 0.28 7.2 —
peterpasand HIP 54373 b — 0.17299 11.23 — — — —
petti amba 2019 OGLE-2018-BLG-0596 b — 0.19306 0.57 — 6.8 —
rata amba OGLE-2018-BLG-0596 b
vellai colomban 2019 SDSS J1228+1040 b — — — —
willard HR 858 b — 4.9 — 1.13 — 0
boribo muyini HR 858 c — — 3.3569866 0.0382 4.2 —
dodo HR 858 d 0.55 1.136 4.5 — 3100 —
mawazo KMT-2018-BLG-1990L b 0.229 — 835 — —
sindano KMT-2018-BLG-1292 b
jin hwang MOA-bin-29 b
red jin hwang NGTS-5 b 2019
tainong n 1 OGLE-2018-BLG-0740L b
khaew sawei
nam dok mai
rad
brahm kai meu
okrong
haden
keitt
kent
tommy atkins
cao lanh cat chu
binh dinh elephant
hoa loc sand

NGTS-5 b 2019	60	—	22482	—	0.42	—
OGLE-2018-BLG-0740L b	—	—	10790	9.75	0.25	—
21 Sco b	—	—	34.5558	0.2068	0.085	89.89
HD 221420 b	0.595	0.91	17.085	0.1293	0.105	88
HD 92987 b	0.082	0.767	649.918	1.487	0.24	—
TOI-216 c	—	—	25.2	0.143	0.15	—
TOI-216 b	—	—	3.2498	0.041	0.14	—
HD 210193 b	—	—	3090.9	4.074	0.11	—
HD 211970 b	—	—	120.878	0.439	0.19	—
HD 39855 b						
HD 102843 b						
HD 103949 b						
WASP-175 b 2019	0.99	1.208	3.0652907		0.044	0	85.33
WASP-171 b 2019	1.084	0.988	3.8186244		0.0504	0	88.3
WASP-169 b 2019	0.561	1.304	5.6114118		0.0681	0	87.9
WASP-182 b 2019	0.148	0.85	3.3769848		0.0451	0	83.88
HD 206255 b	—	—	96.045	0.461	0.23	—
HD 21411 b	—	—	84.288	0.362	0.4	—
HD 64114 b	—	—	45.791	0.246	0.12	—
HD 8326 b	—	—	159	0.533	0.2	—
HD 24085 b	—	—	2.0455	0.034	0.22	—
HIP 71135 b	0.0227	0.1516	87.19	0.335	0.21	—

TOI-402 b
NGTS-6 b 1.33 1.271 4.75642 0.05245 — 88.36 —
KIC 10544976 (AB) b 2019 — 0.882058 0.016623018 0
HD 181234 b 2019 — — — 6136 6.56 0.29 —
HD 25015 b — — 7462.06 7.52 0.73 — —
K2-32 e — 0.0901 — 6019 6.19 0.39 — —
HD 213885 c — 4.34882 0.04951 — —
K2-294 b 2019 — — 24.16 0.1344 — —
K2-293 b 0.1472 4.78503 0.056798 — —
HD 213885 b 0.02778 0.2186 2.50387 0.036 0 —
Qatar-9 b 2019 1.19 0.15568 13.1225 0.1 — 85.5 —
Qatar-10 b 0.736 1.009 1.008035 — 88.8 —
Qatar-8 b 0.371 1.534 1.540731 0.02012 0 80.09
WASP-177 b 0.508 1.285 1.645321 0.0234 0 89.23 —
TOI-270 d 2019 0.017 1.58 3.71495 0.0286 0 85.87 —
TOI-270 b 0.006 0.19 3.071722 0.0474 0 89.29 —
WASP-181 b 2019 0.299 0.11125 11.38014 0.0733 0.03957 — 84.14
WASP-183 b 2019 0.502 1.184 3.36008 0.0306 0 89.69 —
1.47 4.5195064 0 88.65 —
4.1117771 0.04632 0.05427 —
85.37 88.38 —

concretions and natural history

if you say that beneath the curve of my shoulder there's a whole railway station
a depot with solids and voids		it's a matter
of holding each other in the dark		of seeking that point in the hand of another
where a vein or a tendon are not just bodies
but moving clusters
human events		trees and seasons

because falling is a choice and a learning
that takes place only in the bodies of others
the point in which something binds itself and binding opens
to the motions that unite the living beneath the vault of space

this form of falling and no other
this bare collective sliding can tell us
how the beginning sounded	the story of those who
passed through the arch of darkness	wanted to be touched
at the carpet's edge		at the meadow's end

to hold therefore	is	to hold together
this is the task given to us above the void
the story of the clusters that in spite of everything		you say
in spite of everything	are vein and naked meadow
single body and space		humans and trees in motion

Rihamuddin lives on the streets and has nothing but time
one time between the fourth and six years of his life he walks looking for food
lit up like the others by a sun he isn't thinking of

and traverses together with light lots of other things one explodes
an ape electrocuted on a high-voltage power pole
falls beside him with a dull thud

some surprised people come out from the shops although this happens often
Rihamuddin sees that the ape is curled up on the ground
with eyes closed but a paw twitches imperceptibly

he's watching the other kids by the minaret and other events oc-
cur in an undefined frame Rihamuddin now has a wife another
abandoned woman and he drives a tuk-tuk through the city centre's unpaved streets

when he can he stops and buys food for his past drinks some tea
thinks of his children apes walk up between the power poles
and the membrane of smog changes colour layer by layer above the city

Mrs. Maxwell cleans a condominium in which she doesn't live
one morning in the subway she happens to think the following

or maybe one day a word could occur beyond
darkness and light   to liberate events from causes
going home   people later   and she asks herself
but it's no longer a question   it's a line
a galaxy cluster   a quasar that shines in the distance

Mrs. Maxwell has opened the glass door and now stands on her knees
at the bottom of the stairs she chooses the detergents she needs

Cif
Ajax
Viakal
Lysoform
Quasar
Sun
Ariel
WC-Kleen

she notices a wedge of sun slowly extending
over the floor

“ever since I started working at the slaughterhouse I don’t feel anything anymore
less every day   I get up at 5 in the morning   on the edge of town
asking for nothing   and I leave for work already wanting the day to be over
but today the wind loudly moves every single leaf
an insect passes buzzing in the sunny quiet everything changes
I’m afraid of being out of work but I’ll find something

on the station platform I choose the door half-closed on the dark
from which comes out the fresh moist odour typical of a construction site
the flowers outside
the dusky shadow that moves   the wood at the plant’s exit
though gloomy   makes this moment tolerable”

he looks old in the glass
and an object cracks
the bud is bruised   changes its look
adapts

Samira is a 15 year old girl
in 2016 she was kidnapped held in captivity and *sold to at least three different*
people
who beat her up and sexually assaulted her
before being forced into marriage and giving *birth to a child*
her husband was killed in coalition bombing
and Samira fled with her child into the camp of

some nuts reproduce by falling from a tree
into the ocean and then floating
on the surface of the water for several months
before they wash ashore
and germinate

Peter fled alone
separated from his aunt and his sister he lived in the bush with other displaced people
he was ten *an armed group recruited him*
teaching him to load and shoot cook wash clothes
and carry equipment

in the informal settlement each toilet is *shared by more than 100 people*
many adults have resorted to using diapers *at night*
to avoid having to leave their tents and *wait in line*
for the toilet in the dark

ovoid structures hang from the top of a tree
offscreen

and since he said "now I'm pissing myself" and wanted to be brought down
he was brought down and then he said "now I'm shitting myself" and was
conveyed to the latrine and then brought before the lords and
and given that the aforementioned Brother Tommaso Campanella
interrogated by the lords as to his name he replied
stood in complete silence he didn't move a muscle and it seemed
"my name is Brother Tommaso Campanella"
as if he felt no pain

for now they have no choice but to wait
for now they have no choice but to wait

if a dragonfly flies free from these leaves

we hide in the corners of the rooms
we hide in the corners of the rooms

often a decade is more felt than known
by the colour of images of a photo or a videoclip
that seem different from the present   only at a distance

what the 2000's were is still hard to say
much less the 10's or the 20's   whereas we can begin to define
the 90's by the dull pastel of films on VHS
and the 80's are now clear to everyone   between Terminator Thatcher
boxy shapes and neon fabrics

and while films   even the remotest   can last
memory by contrast evolves   and that's how we go back
in our mind to the backyard   that doesn't speak
the rusty metal drying rack shivers slightly
in the wind   the concrete floor is burnt   deserted
and the cracks from which grass and moss emerge seem
for an instant   births and messages

at the height of an insect buzzing in the mid-air
child
or of an observing animal
the passages are shadows   silent legs   a pole and a pail
in a corner   it's useless to keep walking   like that faceless man
around a space that lies   some say
behind a house on the edge of town

everything would remain undefined even from that perspective
a warm and cloudy afternoon mutates in the mind but not in time
nor in the colour that the objects   slanting   take on through the refraction
of a light deflected by changes   obstacles   invisible gravitations
and by the various forms of time and of the void

you might as well   at times   ask the day and the years
seek to make their rotation something lived
now   instead of a lag or a hitch in perception

rubber mass   rubber mass
rubber mass left at the entrance and never considered again
rubber mass that unites the body with the mind
the nature with the artefact   rubber mass do not abandon us

while hands eyes and days
and in a dull-coloured photo from some port
a palm tree waves in a planter
while people argue on television

near a brick arch in a suburban park
beneath the yellow sun of late afternoon
an aggregate of matter waits without saying anything
condenses a part of the whole without judging
or asking   its joy is being
mass   motion   void   and energy

“we were searching all over for a system
a causal link between them and the leaves
does a tree remember yesterday’s breeze?
it dreams of numberless phenomena   indistinct   unremarked
it could have been worse   it could have had weight
to crush things more and more every morning
until it flattens the choices and subtracts the sun
as a point of origin and message without subject
and us exposed in the midst of this current   but now distant
without knowing how to move forward
after we’ve already looked everywhere”

and suddenly there's just one person in the room
albeit with rapid flashes   at intervals   another appears
in the mind   sitting on the edge of an armchair   like an
antique wonder at the colours of the plastic and the glass
discovered on a shore from the past

sometimes you want   in the evening   to evade the night
says a man of uncertain age   with modest clothes
leaving a condominium
to come to terms with the day already done
as if it could be tomorrow
to recompose the voids and the bottles   to accept the readymade errors
to discover that between one branch and another moves more than just the void

how long will the joy last this time   how long will this
wave last   Mrs. Maxwell asks herself
when we meet by the elevator

a transfer tickles my peripheral vision

who is it?

I am dark matter
I have come to tell you that that night
on the bridge you could have acted differently
maybe it would have been less fair toward others
but surely more authentic

things we lose in this universe
are they perhaps found again in another?

I can’t tell you that
in any case you wouldn’t understand structures and relations
so different from those to which you’re too accustomed

you speak in a kind of bookish way
but by the by why do you speak
and how can you speak?

to this there is likewise no response that you
could presently understand

I cling to memory
for example to the recollection of our
bodies that at that moment weren’t then able
to draw close or of his ambiguous look
as long as I live that at least will remain

do what you want but if you like memory
then always remember that your individual life
is only the smallest part
of all of life to which you have always
and will always belong

amen so at some point
I’ll be united with you
when my individual life is over?

an individual life is always over
and even if for the moment you don’t feel it
always taken as you are with yourself
I’m already crossing through you

we are one single skin the unknown
only scares those who want
control

note only apparently banal
many artefacts are imitations
of natural things   helicopters of dragonflies
airplanes of birds   swords siphons and containers

but no organic body possesses interchangeable pieces
snakes and mantises change their skin like jackets
but they can't put it back on   fruit falls and it is impossible
to hang it back up   not even on other branches
and no animal can part with an antenna or a limb
and then put it back in a different place

not even stones   after being pulled up   can
substitute parts of the surface   from which they were pulled
with the same precision as tubes in a motor
or in a hydraulic system   or as the feet
of a refrigerator   or as the pedestal
of a lamp   as propellers   as fans

(but some wounds can heal over   some tentacles regrow)

two overlapping insects
as if it were possible to decompose one's body
into agglomerations of particles and to mix it
with architectural elements   or with a moment
of intense green

as if it were possible to pass through barriers at the airport
while you move away through the security checks

The Converted Plant

before we searched among the ruins now in the facades before it was a matter of tracing trajectories now of traveling them before of traversing an object in the grass now of traversing the grass with this object before of drawing growths now of digging holes before of digging holes now of producing growths before a container held our lunch now we buy ourselves lunch in a box the story has changed but changes

beneath the grass's convex moisture
above

and they too should have seen this opaque sun searching searching to become part of the vertical landscape searching for the line of the vertical landscape before the movement toward the inside of the cylinders behind the diaphragm that had carried them from the other side to look for the line of the vertical landscape in the opaque sun that emanates from the hills nearby mineral hills coated with a dark shiny skin like the cylinders within which they rotated all together with their families and the evenings passed in front of the rooms before resuming the circular rhythmic gesture in place of the machines these organic machines coated in a dark shiny skin like the mineral hills where they were all walking together with their families and the Sundays spent waiting for the opaque sun and the return of the vertical landscape behind the diaphragm behind the pulse of heat at the height of the machines at the height of the hills at the height of this chemical sun and of its noise which is now the story of those who are left on the other side of the landscape to wait for the machines to trace the circular gesture the mineral gesture within the cylinders dark and brilliant like history's skin this liquid skin this skin of water that doesn't rotate anymore now it doesn't rotate anymore but unmoving it reflects the base of the cylinders to the point of redoubling them to the point of pushing them into the earth into space's dark skin a mineral space pushed beneath the machines coated by buildings without history by facades darker than the sun that illuminates them with its slanting light every evening every Sunday before resuming its circular gesture in place of the machines behind the hills around gutted and flattened by machines constructed by other machines beyond the hills around from the other part of the landscape by other stories by the same story the story of the hills gutted and flattened for the families and the evenings and the Sundays spent waiting for the opaque sun and the return of a landscape without matter and without machines and yet vertical above the skin of water that unmoving reflects these buildings without history and the other side of the landscape as the sky filters through space with its opaque sun with the silent sound of its opaque sun that reflects on the shiny dark surface of people and of machines of cylinders and of hills of history's evenings this story that is like a skin into which are inserted buildings displacements and perhaps despite everything new stories and new circular gestures horizontal and mineral narrowings behind the hills gutted and flattened beneath the skin of the landscape without matter in the reflection of the machines on the surface of the water surface that does not rotate the liquid surface of waiting the surface of the buildings that pulse in the heat of the diaphragm in the heat of the opaque circular sun that we see on the facades and that they too saw from a point in their mineral horizontal history them and us together beneath the universal skin of space

up to the distribution of drops during the fall into the hole

up to the agglomeration of the drops in the container   outside the container   up to the distribution of the drops outside the container   to the agglomeration of the drops outside the container   to the fall of the container   to the crumbling of the walls of the container   up to the hole in the hill   to the penetration of the landscape   to locate or to remove according to the distribution of gestures through the centuries   up to the discovery of the hole   to touch the weak walls around the mineral walls   up to the membranes of the container in the factory   to cover the mass   to push the energy to the sides as in a black hole   the black hole of the mass of centuries and of space   the opaque membranes of the factory   the porous walls penetrated by the dark mass of an enormous drop   or of an agglomeration of falls

behind the curtain

she's taking a shower   several forces converge in space this morning   I hear her talk and it isn't like other times   rethink the agglomerations   the trajectories   before the horizon   in the sound of the water flowing now tomorrow   because then she won't be here   I will only find her later with the kids   beneath the kitchen's yellow light at the day's end   she won't be there when the flow is dark and dense in the bottom of the pit of days   and what caresses now in an hour will be that which pushes and controls   to make the lines and objects slide into the expanse of the building and of the mornings   an origin for all the gestures beneath the dark shiny skin of the pit of days beyond the curtain where she was speaking from when the sun was still inside beyond the room where I saw her when her body was still inert before awakening   this factory like her body this morning   this factory like a reply   like a dense flow   like a birth   that   as in nature   isn't chosen by the one who is born

As If They Had Never Been (Seen)

"I want to pay tribute to an error I made   the door of the hotel room opens and the video camera sweeps a hallway in a POV shot   the observer on the other side of the screen follows this trajectory and enters into a modern room in a middling hotel with plastic-coated wooden furniture and a bed on the edge of which are two people   the video camera slows and then stops moving in a frontal position   questions are asked to which they cannot initially respond   then from a few uncertain smiles jumbled words come out in a low voice   they don't even know how to behave in front of the video camera   where to begin

nor do they really know whether they have chosen to meet there but money was promised to them   they know they can produce digital information in the form of agglomerations the authenticity of which however they do not know (nor perhaps will they ever know)   their body is half-controlled and probably this process began in a remote time and place

their skin stretches out only on the outside for the interest of observer 1   situated behind the video camera   and of observer x   situated behind the screen   this information will be sold or perhaps freely shared after an ad to pay for it   it will reach an undetermined number of people who will know where to look and it will change their psychosomatic arrangement   their vegetative structure   I don't know how to explain it to you   maybe I want to say the capacity for empathy of the observers who will receive this sequence   it's only ever a question of information that penetrates memory which in turn produces information on an internal or external area of the body regarding observer 1 I can't comment except to say that his voice   when he asks questions and makes comments   points to something lost forever

although not able to judge the nature of this representation of a state of reality or a series of events   perhaps without even realising it there's a point of no return   one remote movement too many and lacking choice   or awareness   or a fold however minimal in a bit of fabric seen too many times   put it however you want   from which point it will be much harder to rise again without moving unless it is not declared to be the last [*sic*   • part of the message was probably lost]

in the wake of the incident after the data stream   I mean once everything has been switched off   we can only make hypotheses   perhaps observer 1 resumed going down the hallway after paying them in the local currency   and after transmitting this information they will have exited from whatever room it was but only provisionally   they will have said goodbye according to protocol   after all they probably had never met before   each will have gone to eat in a fast food restaurant   believing that they chose the time given to them   or perhaps wanting to celebrate   or who knows maybe to forget an event that will manifest in them in other ways rendering them incapable of falling when they want to but on the other hand more exposed to a constant and irreversible fall to one of the most hazardous forms of loss when we aren't conscious of losing and we think we have gained when in reality on account of the nature of time itself at least with respect to our human scale a piece of content is impossible to take back once it's been given away I don't mean as property but as a form for the hole that's inside many of us and surely inside of them yes as I was saying before lost forever the whole generated by who knows which previous sequences to which not even they have access any more maybe the observers x who will have seen and not lived those events will be able to distance themselves even if in a painful progression from this sequence of organic data refreshing the screen won't be enough I think it'll be necessary to go out and ask for help from the trees and from someone who has this kind of information

it won't be necessary to describe the events in detail a few unstable coordinates will be enough to orient oneself in a space that will nonetheless remain invisible and perhaps some will be saved only then will one be able to speak of freedom of democracy and of similarly big things anyway now I've got to hang up and go I hope to talk again but not to see you ever again in front of me as if you were an extension of needs neither perceived nor recognised alright I will try to have to hand as many dimensions as possible at the moment of our encounter and the waves that spread into some of them let's hope that "

[at that point the static drowned out the rest of the conversation it seemed just about over anyway what do you think?]

concretions and natural history

albedo *(from the latin albedo* whiteness) refers in botany
to the internal layer generally white in colour
typical of the citrus rind

albedo (from the latin *albēdo* whiteness) of a surface
refers to the fraction of light or incident solar radiation
that is reflected in all directions

therefore this indicates the reflective power of a surface
the exact value of the fraction depends *for the same material*
on the wavelength of the radiation in *question*

if the word albedo is used without further *specification*
it is understood to refer to visible light

or

o r

o

⊕

⊙

I'm getting hit in the face and later I hear shots and a faraway cry
I'm scared I'm cold I don't know what to do

now I don't feel anything

or

soap bubbles slowly oscillate in the air
while I hold my mother's hand in the park
we watch their trajectory a few on the way down hit the grass or
a bush exploding without a sound

different kinds of waves and light produce events   they are deflected by objects
and are not made to be heard or seen
the senses decompose signals into data to make them into matter
according to inherent criteria   but with other senses these motions
would have behaved in different ways

radiation does not require intentionally designed
detectors   other invisible phenomena
occur only in the presence of an observer
who can be without sense organs   so every shining berry hanging
on its bush reflects not all things but everything
even when no one passes
and a zone of nonexistent sun lingers on a bird's feather

just as the deer longs *for the fountains*
so a strawberry bush descends from a terrace in search of dirt
it can hold on to   sending a part of itself to explore down below

the sound of people's voices
mixes with the sound of drops' voices
and maybe it's no longer necessary
to return to that hotel room to retrieve
something left on the table   by the green lamp

the external membrane and shell of an egg
must be porous enough to let gas and nutrients pass through
and strong enough to protect life
at least that is the accepted interpretation
of a causal link

but in other areas power authorizes ruptures
disappearances and identities   military actions decisions and displacements
for which in the end it does not know the reasons

it's that below   we are told   covered by the suburban onramp
hemmed in by the trees' blurred canopy
there's a river made of void and everything
even if sometimes when getting out of bed
it seems that the ceiling gets lower
and the stairs hang in the mirror

or on the other hand   because there's always another hand
a protein-based history of being
aggregated fruits for example and that which pushes

the drupes   the follicles   the achenes   to hold together
the Sumerian man of green stone to last
uninterruptedly   for four thousand years   observing events and people
without needing pupils   now from a museum display case
even when it’s thought and not presence
that brings us to him

it’s time to enter into the big soup kitchen
where the hungry cook their food together   offered unconditionally
and they eat it sitting on the ground in a long row from one side of the space to the other
then they stack the plates and trays   and they wash them in the same position

it’s time to widen the room into an expanse
and for the expanse to turn itself into morning grass sun   extension
of concept and substance within thought
where almost nonexistent things revolve   put
someplace   but without a location   and as a result often
unnoticed

PSR B1620-26c is an extrasolar planet *orbiting*
around the pulsar PSR B1620-26 in the M4 *globular cluster*
it was discovered the 10th of July 2003 *on the basis of information*
provided by the Hubble space telescope
the hoverfly hangs in the air near my hat
we ask ourselves what it's watching but a sure response
is not given we forgot the water
can you go back in and buy a few bottles?
the planet is about 12400 light years away from the Solar System
it has a mass double that of Jupiter
and is probably around 13 billion years old

PSR B1620-26b was probably formed
before the stars of Population II endowed with sufficient mass
necessary to form a disc of protostellar material
orbiting around a parent star
in which planetary formation was possible
Mutterbranch treemother Mutterbranch treemother
Mutterbranch treemother Mutterbranch treemother
and the sounds of plants and birds when you close your eyes but above all
a continuous penetrating frequency that we could perhaps call
the sound of the sun
the presence of such elements in the oldest *astral bodies*
has led to the hypothesis of the existence of a *Population III*
of high-mass stars the collapse of which *would have produced the nuclear*
reactions necessary for fusion
I have to put the car in the garage
I have to get a new phone the screen broke
I have to call the doctor back for my prescription
I have to renew my gym membership
I have to go and get my clothes from the cleaners
alternatively *it's* possible
that PSR B1620-26b was originally a star
that then for various reasons lost parts of its own mass
shots cries and running close to the dust behind the bulkhead
under a blinding light
PSR B1620-26c was the first circumbinary *planet*
discovered with pulsar timing *the two stars are*
a neutron star and a white dwarf
making it also the first object
in orbit around a white dwarf
some knots of light link up behind your eyelids
when sun filters through the skin outside the tents
of the refugee camp for once maybe
some of us will be able to feel only those
abstract forms made by rays in the eyeballs
or in the brain rather than hands that tear and poke
PSR B1620-26 is also the first *planet to be found*
inside a globular cluster

of forgiveness   of coagulation
of soap whose colours are observed in the transparency
of some bubbles that move through the air

of struggles for liberty   of groups   of injustices and classes
of abuse   of power that hides itself in us
even when we don’t think we’ve ever suffered it or sought it

of all of this the orbits and oscillations
of a blackberry bush speak without talking
while birds say something else
and make noise as they speak

a bag is filled up with air   the wires are interwoven
where the stalk bends toward something
we could call light

or in masses of tissues and nerves   in the embrace of
reconciliation   when things said or done
count less than the nameless aggregate that maybe   listen   maybe
persists even inside the fruit
placed on a dish   by the window

note give a certain importance to aquatic plants
to their weave and among the poles
through the window of a train or grouped in vats
cross-sectioned parks from the mind of an electrician
or a gardener in a provincial city
who ask for help from inside an armoire
while they could slowly sink down the declivity
touching the container’s liquid surface there are
two options go down and intertwine
climb up the plane
think density despite the pane

pumps normally want need to function with negative pressure
the low pressure level in the inflow or suction pipes
wants needs to remain below 0.4 bar at full load

and at the lowest water level
the speed of the flow in the suction pipes wants needs not to
exceed 2.0 m/s for a Qca flow rate

every pump wants needs to be equipped with emergency diversion pipes
that may guarantee at partial capacity at least 1% of the flow
as cooling water

a testing pipe wants needs to be located on the delivery pipe
above the alarm valve in such a way as to permit
regular tests of the pump at full capacity

every pump wants needs to have a dedicated pipe for inflow
or suction to which no other device
is allowed wants to be connected

the pumps' characteristics want need to be constant
and to include the actual values according to the following
formula (p+0.4 bar 1.2 • Qca)

does a jellyfish decide to be carried by the current
or does it simply let itself be carried?
is there a difference between these two propositions?

could it be that a jellyfish is diffident
when faced with the unknown waters
like we are before an invisible horizon?

suddenly a power pole seen from the moving train
appears to be denser in volume and history
a few trees form a blurred canopy

a line dissolves   leaving space to space
while the thin stalk of hops keeps climbing up a pole
day after day   in spite of everything

even at those points on the edge a relation can occur
between masses of matter
that light up the internal layers of objects
between bodies

and I conceive the morning while you talk to me how to ask for help
the branch in the water that would speak the whole movements of people planets
seasons how the light is made oblique by the clouds
and thus traces language onto things here as elsewhere
beings and objects united under the infinite skin of space

or empty		or full	black hole or orifice
or like a planet	a bubble	a rock		an orange
or an orbit	a letter		a ring	a carousel
a circular source where water quivers
because of the imperceptible movements of the ground
an indecisiveness		an alternative	an exclamation
a way back			in circular motion

to this lingering scent of the seasons

Letter to the Unobservable

dear friends the carousel has gone round here for a long time if one can still speak of time since space is a room without coordinates one of you said once I remember that if nothing means anything everything means something and the void exists for us in a series of strata in the deep then as something that could be called matter

that's how a moth's unforeseeable flight by a lightbulb suddenly seemed to me in the evening after dinner like writing of in the dark its trajectories signifying in a way altogether different from these words

similarly the movement of a rush in the water and the way it vibrates more intensely when a dragonfly perches on top of it don't explain anything don't foretell anything and yet they support this language and beat out the rhythm of the thought that will arrive from my body maybe all the way to your minds or will stay in the sand like a sound and that will be just fine

dear friends I'm sorry to have let you leave in the yellow afternoon light through the vineyards sloping toward the summer's end to go back in the house and wait for the rain that will beat on the roof and the glass every drop a concept or an event

in fact friends I would like deep down for you to forgive me without asking for anything in return and for you to accept my faults unconditionally I would like to be loved by you even if the wind may change the orientation of things and show a side of them never seen before

I would like for you to have no more regrets for your eyes even if tired out by the body's heat and by the years to be able to see every molecule every particle that in orbit composes the objects given to our experience without a specific reason or necessity beyond the fact that they are here and we are here

but above all friends I would like for you to hold on to one another leaving no one out for you to be a home for each other and rain that comes down along the curve even from the dark and unobservable part where parallel lines can still converge if we look and look for each other if only in the name of a knowledge without understanding

I can't cast away the possibility of knowing us all of us still water and sun rather liquid and light landscape and horizon formed within every wave or drop or branch moved by the breeze and exposed at a new angle I can't not hope to find you among these photos scattered in front of me taken in the summer we will all be together at home friends peace freedom are scary we've learned it at a price and these words may seem banal in the eyes of some but maybe not of those who have chosen to return to that basket full of pomegranates stones forms of thought

in the end as you all know it's a matter of walking slowly over the layer of black algae attached to the rocks and turning toward the canopy of the trees that swelling up look out of focus renouncing the easy rules of remote vision it's perhaps in this letter that I've chosen to send you a matter of possibly saving ourselves

dear friends I miss you even if I don't know who you are and I hope that you will return while I wait if since time is a room without coordinates one can speak of waiting I won't stop thinking of you as lines of clouds on the curve of a horizon seen from above and circuits of light around a gravitational field or stones gathered on a shore flooded with the slanted rays of late afternoon

e agglomerati,
degli alberi

o

concrezioni e storia naturale

il buio del sonno corrisponde forse al nero dello spazio
per qualche ora fuori dalla propria condizione di individuo
un muretto di calce tracciava un perimetro
attorno a un giardino vuoto   anzi pieno ma di terra scura
confida una persona qualsiasi ad un'altra   sedute al tavolo della mensa
in pausa dal lavoro   poi mentre mi lasciavo andare ad uno stato
di pericolo animale   imminente e senza contorni definiti
quella stessa area si è riempita molto velocemente
con fiori selvatici tendenti al bianco e al giallo chiaro
e di tante forme e lunghezze diverse
mentre la parte esterna rimaneva fuori fuoco
e come accartocciata benché liscia

per lungo tempo   risponde l'altra   la parte esterna
non si è differenziata   così la sottraevo
alla mia percezione   e visto che non era interamente
altra rispetto a me   io ero inconoscibile anche a me stesso a
perché non ero altro a da me né dentro di me
e il mondo non era   fuori di me   ma ci sono stati
e condizioni nei quali ci si porta talora senza saperlo
dove qualcosa   un merlo nell'erba   un ramo mosso
dalla corrente   ci salva   anche se non è una
salvezza senza conseguenze

andando a fare la spesa in un supermercato meno caro
aggiunge una terza persona di mezza età sedendosi di fronte   ancora
con la cuffia igienica ed i guanti   suo a figlio a in cerca di lavoro
la moglie
il marito sempre davanti alla televisione   abbiamo imboccato
per sbaglio un sentiero lungo alcune villette in costruzione
sono bastati pochi metri e il canto (o era un discorso?) degli uccelli
ha reso la vista degli ambienti esterni fuori fuoco
e come accartocciati benché lisci   mentre dove eravamo
noi erano solo versi di animali ormai   e riccioli di rami
foglie e fiori in moto   aggregati minerali
inquadrati dall'arco di un cespuglio di more   dei fagiani
si muovevano sul prato di fronte come concetti   come nubi interstellari

è ora   le li interrompe qualcuno che passa accanto a loro
di tornare a lavorare   batte con l'indice sul quadrante senza lancette
del suo orologio da polso   poi si allontana   nel buio dello spazio
le stagioni e gli individui ruotano in successione
sfumando l'una nell'altra   in questo come in altri pianeti inclinati
gli uni negli altri

la vite *per diversi caratteri* è molto diversa dalle altre viti
ha fusto *adulto rugoso* (come zigrinato) di colore grigio
ma la *corteccia non si sfalda* come nelle altre viti
ha *viticci sempre e solo* singoli (mai ramificati) sottili e robustissimi
e una *forte tendenza* alla femminellatura

i grappoli sono disordinati e di norma con 6-8 fino a 40 acini
gli acini sono piuttosto grandi a buccia spessa e dura
che non è inghiottita al consumo
spesso gli acini maturano separatamente gli uni dagli altri
e si staccano singolarmente dal grappolo

le foglie sono piuttosto piccole (15-18 cm) non sono mai lobate
ma tonde con una grossolana dentatura molto sottili e lucide

la pianta ha frutti (acini) di colore nero (blu-rossiccio) *o bronzeo*
molto raramente di colore rosso
Il diametro degli acini (sempre sferici o solo *leggermente ovati)*
spazia dai 13 ai 38 mm
a maturità gli acini si distaccano con *estrema facilità*

la abscissione (distacco) del grappolo è *molto difficile*

il tonfo inatteso di un frutto   la discesa graduale di una foglia
sono forme di torsione del flusso   modi di manifestazione tra i tanti
che possono accadere anche senza presenza
e quando non ci saremo   quelle stesse traiettorie
restituiranno corpo al corpo   unione all'aggregato

cercando quella pera a forma di cervello tra le foglie vicino allo steccato
è sembrato possibile accettare che le cose siano in movimento
e che certi errori non saranno ripagati
se non dalla visione simultanea di un albero come unità
e come gruppo   di oggetti ed eventi

«passato da una mano all'altra al banco del mercato
si agitava nel sacchetto   allungava il collo
cercando l'aria con la testa   e fremevano le ali
io cercavo di spostare ai lati le verdure e le patate
che la mia ospite aveva preso a un altro banco
e lasciato cadere nel sacchetto stesso come se fosse già stato
una pietanza   perché sapevo invece quanto avesse paura
e bisogno di respirare   quanto fosse ancora
attaccato alla vita   senza altra ragione
che la vita stessa   questo sapere
penso adesso   è una conoscenza immediata che
come ogni forma del sentire   è propria ad ogni vivente»

fig. 107 fotografia da vicino di frutti maturi della grevia asiatica
albero le cui foglie sono alterne
peziolate
cuoriformi
rotonde
appuntate
a 5 nervi
quasi lobate
tomentose al di sotto
della grandezza di quelle del melo
fiori in numero di tre
peduncolati
ascellari

hort. angl. g. pelosa
stufa calda

le membrane possono essere preparate nella forma di fogli piani
tubi capillari e fibre cave

i metodi di preparazione delle membrane artificiali sono
per sinterizzazione
per precipitazione da evaporazione
per precipitazione termica
per stiramento da un film polimerico
per estrazione
per via elettrochimica (col processo elettrochimico chiamato etching)

devi svegliarti presto per l'acqua

ho sette bambini e non abbastanza acqua da bere

dobbiamo supplicare i nostri vicini che ci diano acqua da bere

ogni giorno al pozzo le donne si battono per l'acqua

dopo la preparazione le membrane possono essere assemblate in
sistemi a piatto e telaio (con arrangiamento analogo alla filtropressa)
moduli a spirale
moduli a fibre cave
in tubi o fibre da 0.25÷2.5 mm di diametro
assemblate assieme a formare il modulo
in configurazione rettilinea o ad U
moduli tubulari
con tubi di diametro maggiore di 3 mm
in genere assemblati in geometri a fascio tubiero e mantello

le membrane artificiali vengono realizzate con polimeri organici
o con materiale inorganico

polimeri organici polisolfone (PS) polietersolfone (PES)
acetato di cellulosa (CA) poliammide (PA)
polivinildedefluoruro (PVDF) poliacrilonitrile (PAN)

materiali inorganici allumina gamma allumina alfa
vetro borosilicato

le maree solari gravitazionali sono probabilmente
la ragione principale della lenta rotazione
di Venere ma non ne spiegano il moto retrogrado

la documentazione sui tempi di eclisse mostra che il giorno
si è leggermente allungato durante gli ultimi due millenni

l'est del paese accoglie da inizio anno
migliaia di rifugiati in fuga dalle zone di conflitto

arrivati quasi senza niente sono stati progressivamente
condotti più lontano all'interno della frontiera
dove uno spazio è stato attribuito dalle autorità

il campo si estende su alcune centinaia di metri
sono visibili degli operai che stanno martellando una superficie
per la preparazione di un alloggio
degli agenti che verificano i dati dei nuovi arrivati

questo martedì pomeriggio gli abitanti dei villaggi
situati intorno al campo sono venuti a incontrare
i nuovi arrivati offrendo loro viveri e vestiti

« que dieu veille sur nos femmes et enfants
que votre souffrance arrive à terme
que le malade guérisse
que celui qui a tout perdu
retrouve la prospérité
que celui qui est sans abri trouve un toit »

fig. 353 fotografia da vicino delle infiorescenze sferiche dell'albero di neré

questo albero dal tronco dritto e dalla scorza liscia
può misurare 25 m di altezza

il *suo fogliame è caduco* ed è composto da foglie multi-pennate
l'albero *comincia a fiorire* tra 5 e 7 anni
i suoi *frutti sono grandi* baccelli sospesi a grappoli
contenenti chicchi neri rivestiti da una polpa gialla
chiamata nerè   un albero può generare
fino a 100 chicchi all'anno   i frutti cominciano
a maturare subito prima delle prime piogge e continuano
per la maggior parte della stagione

l'albero dispone di una radice-perno in grado di cercare acqua
fino a 60 metri di profondità

l'albero è principalmente impollinato da *pipistrelli*   api
mosche   vespe   *formiche* e *scarabei*
è stato dimostrato che il fogliame del *nerè*
contribuisce alla fertilità del suolo

tre questioni fondamentali

1 le spore e il modo in cui si spostano e si riproducono in particolare
quando la fotosintesi non è possibile

2 il comportamento e la presenza di cose in apparenza immateriali
che si propagano nello spazio

3 quali sono i criteri di decisione di un essere vivente
ad esempio come una pianta che ha fiori di più colori
decide di assegnare questo o quel colore a un tale fiore
oppure perché un uccello posato su un ramo
improvvisamente vola via anche in assenza
di un predatore di cibo o di suoi simili da raggiungere

anche se la nebbia forma una membrana sulla distesa   oltre l'acqua
l'oscillazione delle cime degli alberi può essere condivisa
l'erba invita ad uscire   a prendere parte sotto la neve
si dà nella forma del possibile
un mantello di plastica divelto dai fermagli ondeggia
sotto il ponte di un cavalcavia
togliendo alla vista parti di un'area di sosta

forse non si tratta per una volta di opporsi al reale
di provare a risalire il tempo
vorrei dirti mentre salutandoti chiudo la portiera
e imbocco la strada che sale nel vuoto per riempirlo di legno e rami
forse quel film dietro la massa di materia
è stato girato il giorno in cui saremo tutti insieme   a casa
in ascolto tra stella e lava   oltre l'inizio
mentre una formazione liquida scende incessantemente
di fronte alla luce di un lampione   e sopra le foglie
un passaggio della crescita e non della degenerazione
pomeriggio dello spazio   incastro di stagioni
sotto l'erba   fuori dai giorni
oltre il torrente   dopo la nebbia
gli alberi   oscillano

che cosa succede quando spengo
e il silenzio di sopra mi invade?
non tutta la verità si trova nel camion delle consegne
non tutti i ricordi nella luce che cambia per un movimento
inatteso di nubi

se ci giriamo nel vento brillante tra i rami   i vuoti tra le cose
vanno via   potremo cercare insieme un'estensione
o la superficie ruvida del frutto   e accettare
che qualcosa   a tratti   a segnali   possa morire

dentro l'inizio del bosco il sole è fuori prospettiva
riluce nel buio crescente una massa di oggetti
bianca d'inverno verde d'estate
il passo scricchiola su questa pellicola organica
fatta di strati e passaggi lampioni e concetti
se dici ad esempio che non siamo soli devi calare la corda
nel buco che ci unisce trovare il cibo
con cui accettare il vuoto e riconoscerlo dietro lo schermo
contro la paura una vertigine verticale
corpo che cerca
linguaggio animale
massa di oggetti in espansione orizzontale verde d'inverno
bianca d'estate albero e antenna all'imbrunire
da dove chiamare da dove

«dopo una notte difficile»
«sí»
«lo sguardo si posa sugli oggetti intorno e sul fumo di un camino fuori»
«che filtra in silenzio una collina e le sue case»
una superficie di sole proiettata dalla finestra dipana
un'altra narrazione   il laccio intorno al collo
non impedisce all'animale di girarsi e di notare l'aria
la discesa di abeti   la storia dell'erba
le nubi calmano la vista verticale   la restituiscono al bosco

ti ho visto rovesciare l'infanzia dentro il legno
ritrovare l'aria nel cuscino
e affondare nuovamente nello spazio
gli abeti e i pini come un'orchestra   come gli altri insieme
in ascolto delle stagioni

il vetro copre solo una porzione del giorno
la paura solo una porzione di notte   la neve
solo una porzione di voce

le linee curve della cima   lago e luna   lago a luna
e gli abeti sopra nell'oscurità dànno radici al mattino successivo
la luce del giorno obliqua come le linee curve della cima
lago e luce   lago a luce   il tronco si avvolge ed ispessisce
argilla sotto l'erba sotto neve sotto il salto di un uccello
o il passo di un animale che imbocca lentamente una pendenza
obliqua come la discesa del giorno

sotto gli alberi dentro le radici della notte successiva
un animale respira   si sposta nello spazio
modificando per sempre la distribuzione dell'erba e della terra
prima della notte totale   terra e buio
terra a luce in ogni pendenza dello spazio
sulle linee della cima dove l'erba e la rupe agiscono anche mentre
nessuno passa   anche quando non è osservata
la pietra determina la curva della percezione
e traccia una rete di eventi
radici e pietra   pietra a radici

e agglomerati degli alberi

o

⊙

⊙

⊕

in fisica un corpo nero è un oggetto ideale
che assorbe tutta la radiazione elettromagnetica incidente
senza rifletterla   ed è perciò detto *nero*
secondo l'interpretazione classica *del colore dei corpi*

Tessere

è iniziato tutto da questo bisogno di tagliare la materia   seduto nel peggior bar della città per testare la resistenza della gioia   di fronte ai flipper alle slot machines ai tavoli umidi e alla notizia dell'esodo di migliaia di persone e animali da una qualsiasi altra città   le loro foto in HD con i volti sofferenti sembrano quelle di un documentario o di un set cinematografico il reale occultato sotto l'informazione sotto il resoconto della realtà   eppure si tratta di tenere di restare   di tenere stretto quell'oggetto nell'erba e di sapere anche come lasciarlo andare ma qual è il nostro compito   come possiamo agire senza autodistruggerci   come possiamo aprire la realtà dietro la paura   è certo che il mio compito non è raccontare la mia vita come se fosse più interessante di altre   anche se molti sembrano preferire questa via che non è una via   solo un'illusione di controllo   delle chiazze di neve sono rimaste malgrado la temperatura   malgrado le voci che disturbano il rumore uniforme del treno   queste frequenze elettriche che indicano una continuità tra il nostro mondo e quello della percezione tra il paesaggio e il vuoto tra i due vetri e c'è una differenza sostanziale tra il sasso lavico nero poggiato sullo sterno e il sasso che si forma nello sterno a causa degli altri   del taglio di materia   delle voci che coprono il ronzio uniforme del motore e gli squilli delle macchine nell'erba   attraverso gli alberi   sotto il pendio   dove ci troviamo da dove chiamare   da dove

ed è troppo insipido anche   come hanno fatto in tanti   rifiutare i sentimenti   limitarsi o lasciarsi a una descrizione o pretendere che gli eventi simultanei di una metropoli siano sufficienti a giustificare l'esistenza di una forma di rappresentazione   è vero che noi tracciamo una linea tra le strade o sotto le colline   è vero che una traiettoria non può essere un'altra e forse è proprio questo a fare male   ma come sentire o essere senza scegliere queste architetture senza questo brusio uniforme delle ali degli insetti o del motore dentro l'aria   ogni corpo dotato di movimento o di capacità di crescita   ma anche un sasso o una macchina mossi dalla corrente sono soggetti a una direzione che non è un'altra e se potessimo registrare con una linea di luce tutti i tragitti l'edificio del moto diventerebbe un grumo una massa di materia da tagliare di nuovo per esistere   la vita come causa e fine di questa obliquità   rigonfiamento o dilatazione

uscì   se dico Sofia uscì traccio una linea sopra la linea e ridurre il possibile alla rappresentazione è cosa ben diversa dal saper scegliere   accettare la traiettoria   sapersi cadere in una camera all'indietro nella mia e nella tua testa bambina e in quella di tutti che chiede di dare ascolto in una camera all'indietro che è tutte le camere possibili tutti gli spazi tra gli alberi e nelle uscite oblique   e nei tagli di materia   non c'è Sofia   Sofia è mia figlia che non c'è ancora ed è quindi tutte le figlie possibili tutta la figlia del mondo che siede a un tavolo e fuoriesce da una città assediata e quindi Sofia non è un personaggio   guardatene i tratti in questa foto che non è mostrata perché non è mostrabile   tocchiamo i suoi capelli vaporosi le cui fibre contengono i tragitti che percorrerà nell'erba e tra i palazzi e io con lei tenterò di ritracciare quanto non mi è stato dato   sapendo che l'edificio del moto   che gli spazi tra gli alberi   che la camera all'indietro non è la stessa inclinazione nel taglio della materia e che non possiamo scegliere la nostra stessa nascita   ma possiamo invece scegliere di nascere e cadere

Sofia prese le chiavi la borsa e uscì di casa   sul pianerottolo si sentì come se qualcuno l'avesse tirata fuori dalla porta   come se non fosse stata lei da sola a varcare la soglia   la signora Marconi stava come al solito passando uno straccio bagnato sulle scale di finto marmo   si salutarono cordialmente e con un lieve e indefinito senso di sospetto

qui Sofia non è mia figlia che non è ancora stata concepita ma una donna che esiste dentro di me e con cui condivido parti di storia ma non questa storia   Sofia finì di scendere le scale e si infilò nella metropolitana   la linea 2 o 6 non è la linea 1 o 5 e non è come tracciare uno spazio tra gli alberi   Sofia si sentiva dentro e fuori   dentro al vagone tra gli sguardi opachi di una coppia di adolescenti e quelli pieni di vuoti aperti di un uomo anziano e del suo cane   e fuori dallo spazio perché stava tracciando una traiettoria attraverso un moto che però non dipendeva da lei   fece qualche passo nella direzione opposta al senso di marcia poi si disse che non c'era ragione di opporsi sempre al reale

Sofia in quel momento come tutti noi non era solo un volto e un corpo non solo un movimento e un grumo di pensieri e sensazioni   era anche tutto quello che era stata in precedenza tutta la sua esistenza presente di giovane donna di cui anche se avessimo più dettagli non sapremmo niente perché per sapere qualcosa è necessario ricordarsi che siamo pietre costruzioni corpuscolari e stratificazioni neurologiche   animali e non verbali   tutto l'essere di Sofia in vibrazione nella metropolitana   Sofia nuda sotto i vestiti che aveva indossato quel giorno un po' a caso   quel giorno a caso   Sofia che per una scelta arbitraria potrebbe adesso rimanere nella metropolitana per sempre   continuare il tragitto fino a che noi la pensiamo in spostamento nello spazio indotto da un motore elettrico che emette un brusio uniforme a cui si sovrappone ogni tanto la voce sommessa di un uomo anziano seduto di fronte a lei che dice qualcosa al suo cane non si capisce se lo sgrida oppure se le sue sono parole d'amore per quel magma stellare per quel corpo animale quell'intreccio di tessuti a cui appartengono tutti Sofia compresa se decidiamo che non siano personaggi

queste foto   dice la madre di Sofia mentre Sofia è assente perché la sua traiettoria in metropolitana continua in modo indefinito e indecidibile   queste foto   dice la mamma di Sofia mentre le mostra a un interlocutore senza occhi né forma   queste foto sono state scattate quell'estate   quando saremo tutti insieme   a casa   quando Sofia sarà uscita dalla metropolitana   quando gli sguardi opachi saranno diventati pietre lucide per la risacca   colpite dal movimento del mare   quell'estate quando saremo tutti insieme e non ci saranno più conflitti né divisioni né gerarchie   la madre di Sofia e la signora Marconi sono due corpi smisurati in questa temporalità   due corpi senza forma come quello dell'interlocutore   uniti come massa stellare come tessuto animale fuori dalla porta a vetri   lontano dal citofono e dalle scale   sempre più liquido   sempre più permeabile all'aria e alle configurazioni degli atomi esterni   come il mare   come la risacca contro la quale corre Sofia bambina ridendo contro le onde che ancora si dipanano all'indietro nella camera che la mamma di Sofia ha preparato all'uscita della metropolitana Sofia si immagina che l'uomo possa essere eiettato dal vagone prima di raggiungere la prossima fermata   ma cos'è la prossima fermata   cos'è una fermata qual è l'equilibrio da trovare tra l'opporsi al reale e l'iscriversi nel suo flusso dove dobbiamo colpire pensa Sofia con tutto il suo corpo Sofia nuda sotto i vestiti dentro il cervello dietro gli occhi dove possiamo colpire e quando invece ci si può stendere sull'erba nella risacca dentro casa ora che Sofia è uscita che si è sentita come se qualcuno l'avesse tirata fuori dalla porta giù per le scale ma via da quale casa

Sofia si sentiva dentro e fuori dentro e fuori dalla signora Marconi appena incrociata dentro e fuori da sua madre che non vedeva ormai da qualche millennio Sofia tracciava una linea un vettore nella città ma senza direzione senza temporalità perché Sofia è un insieme di categorie mobili è il movimento della risacca che abbraccia e liscia le pietre è la culla da cui veniamo tutti e per questo il ricordo di qualcosa che non è ancora accaduto e di un evento passato passato senza nome

Sofia non ha un nome e la signora Marconi non ha un cognome   la mamma di Sofia avrebbe un nome ma non lo ha finché non è scritto e se fosse scritto non lo avrebbe più ci troviamo dentro oggetti indefiniti e non ancora accaduti linee di possibile tra gli occhi ancora chiusi questa mattina mentre mi abbracci nel letto e mormori un messaggio di inizio

Sofia non parla nessuna lingua che si possa capire respira forte
sorride come una bambina come un animale

portarla a comprare dei palloni nel parco

è

e

tessere

Inventario di tutte le specie esistenti di mango e dei nomi e caratteristiche di alcuni esopianeti recentemente scoperti

B74
brooks
haden
irwin
keitt
kensington pride
kent
nam doc mai
palmer
R2E2
ashini
fazli
himsagar
khirshapat
langra
lokhon-bhog
raj-bhog
aug din
ma chit su
sein ta lone
shwe hin tha
coquinho
haden
manga espada
manga rosa
palmer
tommy atkins
cambodiana
ameliorée du ...
mango blanco
amélie
black (blackie)
bombay
dou-douce
east indian
graham
haden
julie (st. julian)
long
madame francis
rose
spice-box
starch
baiyu
guixiang
huangpi
huangyu
macheco
sannian
yuexi
haden
irwin
keitt
mora
tommy atkins
ambassador
alfonso
ataulfo
criollos
haden
julie
keitt
kent
reina
tommy atkins
alfonso
hindi
hindi besennara
beid el agl
oweisi
fuss oweis
taymoor
zebdiah
apple
carabao
kinalabaw
indian
piko
pano
panohutan
haden
kent
tommy atkins
francine (madame francis)
muscas
labiche
baptiste
rosalie
poirier
corne
lil
chausa
dusehri
gaddamar
ottu mangai
mulgoba
langra benarsi
badshahpasand
surkha
lofapuri
fajli
hisan nara
alphonso
amrapali
badami

					—		—
						—	79
					—	0	—
					0.0143	1.18	89
			10.57415		—	0.0007	—
			0.7668944	—	0.049	—	
		0.86	0.014		—	89.68	
		1.205	3.778873	—	0.032	89.35	—
TOI-1406 b	46	1.234	2.178	0.1436	0.199	85.37	
NGTS-10 b	2.162	0.107	18.71204	0.231	—	—	—
OGLE-2017-BLG-1434L b	0.725	0.867	55.086	0.0681	0.11		86.8
WASP-143 b	0.0085	0.3551	4.401131	0.141	0.01598	0	—
HD 158259 b	0.244	1.642	24.45		0.31	88.5	—
HD 332231 b	0.12406	—	0.76552398	0.063	0.31	88.5	—
HD 95338 b	21	0.30752	20.902	0.063	0.04394	0.22	87.98
KELT-25 b	—	1.57	20.902		0.07098	0.047	87.43
HD 79211 b	0.12831	1.57	4.066499		0.01782	0	77.18
TOI-849 b	39.3	0.3256	8.350381		0.0318	0	82.01
TOI-1510A b	40	1.5	0.9809734		0.03524	0	80.98
TOI-1130 c	—	2.03	2.0845435		0	88.125	—
HIP 65A b	0.974	1.286	2.2554477	0.0404	—	0.63	—
TOI-157 b	3.213	1.086	3.81433	—	12.2	—	—
TOI-169 b	1.18	0.09707	0.01246		162	—	—
GJS 1815 b	0.791						
OGLE-2018-BLG-0677L b	0.0132						
OGLE-2018-BLG-1339/OGLE-2019/BLG-1019 b			3	—			
KMT-2019-BLG-1953	—	14	0.7683881		0.012	0.064	85.9
TYC 8998-760-1 b	0.00982	0.11883	12.252048		0.077	0.115	89.08
LTT 3780 b	0.0267	0.205	3.9228038		0.04269	0.088	87.08
LTT 3780 c	0.369	1.117	3.1316666		0.03769	0.162	89.58
HATS-47 b	0.243	0.8	4.1480467		0.04515	0.071	88.27
HATS-48A b	0.353	0.765	7.3279474		0.066517		0.013
HATS-49 b	0.1254	0.7224					
HATS-72 b	88.56						
KELT-2019-BLG-1953 c		0.28	—	—	0.8	—	—
KELT-2019-BLG-1953 b		0.59	—	—	0.8	—	—
2MASS J1155-7919 b		10	—	—	582	—	—
HD 191939 b	—	0.3007	8.880411		0.089	—	88.66
HD 191939 c	—	0.2873	28.5806	0.178	—	89.14	—
HD 191939 d	—	0.2819	38.3561	0.216	—	89.49	—
EPIC 249893012 c		0.04616	0.3274	15.624	0.13	0.07	87.94
EPIC 249893012 d		0.03203	0.3515	35.747	0.22	0.15	—
EPIC 249893012 b	0.0145	0.02753	0.174	3.5951	0.047	0.06	86.14
L 168-9 b	0.134	0.124	1.4015	0.02091	0.21	85.5	—
TOI-257 b	—	0.626	18.38827		0.1523	0.24	88.78
TOI-1338	—	1.606	71.4	—	—	—	—
TOI-700 c	—	—	106.341	0.31	0.16	—	—
TOI-700 d	—	—	122.005	0.339	0.29	—	—
HD 158259 c	0.0249	—	11.949	0.079	0.26	—	—
HD 158259 d	0.00406	0.2346	36.052	0.178	0.03	—	—
HD 158259 f	0.00711	0.0901	16.051998		0.0925	—	—
HD 158259 e	—	0.1062	9.977	0.0637	0.032	0.033	88.9
WASP-178 b	—	—	37.426	0.163	0.032	89.67	—
Kepler-65 e	—	—	3.432037	—	—	89.73	—
K2-146 c	1.41	—	5.198	—	—	—	—
K2-198 d	0.82	1.94	12.03	—	—	—	—
	0.02357	0.1954	7.954	—	—	—	—
	—	0.21751	3.3448285	—	—	—	—
			258.8		0.0558	0	—
			4.00498	0.034	0.28	127	85.7
			7.4500177		0.075	87.54	—
					0.05234	—	—
							89.86

bangalora
banganapalli
bombay
bombay green
cheruku rasalu
chinna rasalu
pedda rasalu
fazli
fajri kalan
fernandian
gulabkhas
himayath
himsagar
imam pasand
jehangir
kalami
kesar
kishen bhog
komanga
lalbaug
langra
mafdah
malgis
mallika
mankur
mankurad
moovandan
nattuma
neelum
pairi
priyor
rajapuri
raspuri
ratna
safeda
sammar bahisht
suvarnarekha
totapuri
vanraj
zardalu
alampur baneshan
arumanis
gadung
golek
manalagi
haden
keitt
kent
maya
nimrod
palmer
tommy atkins
kensington pride
glenn
tommy atkins
keitt
maya
van dyke
osteen
kent
patwi
boubo
ngowe
apple mango
apple rumani
arumanis
golek
kuala selangor
malgoa
maha-65
tok hoon
amelie
kent
ataulfo
haden
irwin
kent
manila
palmer
sensation
tommy atkins
van dyke
petakon
oro
criollo
nino
chausa
dusehri
langra
desi
anwar rataul
sindhri
fajri
saroli
bagan pali
alphonso
muhammad wola
neelum
criollos
haden
keitt
kent
tommy atkins
carotte
jose

K2-198 c
K2-198 b
K2-168 c
K2-168 b
2019
K2-43 c
K2-43 b
HD 221416 b
2019
WASP-126 c
2019
WASP-18 c
2019
L 98-59 b
TOI-263 b
PSR J2055+3829 b
2019
CWISEP J1935-1546
HAT-P-70 b
HAT-P-69 b
TOI-125 c
2019
TOI-125 d
2019
TOI-125 b
2019
Borisov
HD 1724 b
2019
Kepler-1661 (AB) b
2019
HD 38677 b
2019
HD 1231 b
2019
HD 42936 b
2019
HD 38677 e
2019
HD 38677 c
2019
HD 38677 d
2019
HD 80653 b
TOI-564 b
TOI-905 b
XO-7 b
2019
OGLE-2013-BLG-0911L b
2019
EPIC 211939692.02
EPIC 211939692.01
USco 1621A b
2019
USco 1556A b
2019
KMT-2019-BLG-0842 b
HIP 36985 b
2019
WD J0914+1914 b
Kepler-154 g
2019
G 9-40 b
OGLE-2016-BLG-1227 b
HIP 41378 g
beta Pic c
AB Dor C b
TOI-677 b
WISE 2150A b
HD 85628 A b
NGTS-8 b
TOI-132 b
OGLE-2015-BLG-1771L b
Proxima Centauri
WASP-185 b
WASP-184 b

		3.3596055		0.03077	—	86.494
	0.12695	17.0428683		0.09083	—	88.904
	0.37372	8.050722	0.0979	0.06231	89.81	—
—	0.11687	15.8523	0.0148	—	—	—
—	0.1659		—	—	89.26	—
—	2.198884	14.2767	0.1228	89.6	—	2019
—	3.471149	0.0201	—	0.115	85.75	—
0.2159	0.836	7.63	—	0.025	—	—
0.4024	—	2.1558		0.009	—	—
0.1904	—	4.989963		0.029392		—
0.202	0.2061	0.556814		0.01	—	86.96
0.1737	0.83	—	0.12959037293		—	
—	39	2019	—	—	—	—
—	11	2.74432452		0.04739	0	96.5
—	1.87	4.7869491		0.06555	0	87.19
6.78	1.676	9.15059	0.0814	0.066	88.54	—
3.58	0.24614	19.98	0.137	0.168	88.795	—
0.02086	0.2614	4.65382	0.05186	0.194	88.92	—
0.0428	0.2432		—	—	3.155	—
0.0299	0.000062				58.6	—
—	—	44926	26.3	0.63	0.06	89.464
50.5	0.053	—	175.06	—	—	—
		18.57	0.1462	0.083	—	—
—	—	5.2049	0.0664	0.083	—	—
—	—	6.6732	0.0662	0.14	—	—
—	—	5.516	0.0651	0.07	—	—
—	—	6.584	0.0733	0.057	—	—
—	—	2.882	0.0422	0.07	—	—
0.0176	0.1439	0.719573		0.0166	—	82.1
1.463	1.02	1.651144	0.02734	0.072	78.38	
0.667	1.171	3.739494		0.04666	0.024	85.68
0.709 1.373	2.8641424		0.04421	0.038	83.45	—
		10.08	—	—	10.8	—
	—	0.232	39.553	—	0.06	—
15	—	0.232	26.8549	—	0.16	—
14	—	—	2880	—	—	—
	—	—	3500	—	—	—
—	10.28	—	—	3.31	—	—
	—	8500	7	0.55	—	—
—	—	—	—	0.07	—	—
0.016	0.9145	1250	—	0.15	—	—
	0.18066	5.746007		0.0385	0	88.57
9.37	—	0.79	—	—	3.4	—
13	—	62.06	0.3227	0.06	—	—
1.236	—	1238	2.72	0.248	97.86	
34	1.179	—	0.58	—	—	
3.1	—	11.2366	0.1038	0.435	87.63	
0.83	1.53	—	341	—	—	
2.9	1.09	2.82406	0.047	0	86.7	
0.07183	1.07	2.4997	0.035	0.01	86.9	
	0.306	4.43527	0.058	0.06	84.1	
0.98	—	2.1097008		0.026	0.087	—
0.57	1.25	0.433	—	—	0.85	84.63
	1.33	—	1894	1.48	0	—
		9.38755	0.0904	0.24	86.8	—
		5.1817	0.0627	0	86.9	

86.494
0.03077 — 88.904
0.09083 — —
0.06231 89.81 —

lucie
auguste
apple mango
arumanis
golek
kaem yao
mangga dadol
alampur baneshan
alice
alphonso
anderson
angie
bailey's marvel
bennet alphonso
beverly
bombay
brahm kai meu
brooks
carabao
carrie
chok anon
cogshall
cushman
dot
duncan
earlygold
east indian
edward
eldon
emerald
fairchild
fascell
florigon
ford
gary
gaylour
glenn
gold nugget
golden lippens
graham
haden
hatcher
ice cream
irwin
ivory
jakarta
jean ellen
julie
keitt
kensington pride
kent
lancetilla
langra benarsi
lippens
mallika
manilita
mendoza
mulgoba
nam doc mai
nam tam teen
neelum
nu wun chan
okrung
osteen
palmer
parvin
pascual
philippine
pickering
po pyu kalay
rosigold
ruby
rutledge
saigon
sensation
sophie fry
southern blush
spirit of '76
springfels
sunset
suwon tip
tepow
toledo
tom dang
tommy atkins
torbert
turpentine
valencia pride
van dyke
zill
hawaiian common
gouveia
hawaiian dwarf
kurahige
mapulehu
momi k
pope
rapoza
sugai
turpentine
fascell
haden
keitt
kent
sensation

0.12695 3.3596055
0.37372 17.0428683 — —
— 0.11687 8.050722 0.0979 — 89.26 —
— 0.1659 15.8523 0.0148 — — 2019
K2-198 c — 2.198884 — 89.6 85.75 —
K2-198 b — 3.471149 0.0201 0.1228 0.115 — —
K2 0.2159 0.836 14.2767 — 0.025 — —
K2-168 c 0.4024 7.63 — 0.009 — —
K2-168 b — 0.1904 2.1558 0.029392 —
2019 K2-43 c 0.202 — 4.989963 0.01 — 86.96
K2-43 b 0.1737 0.2061 0.556814 —
K2-321416 b 0.83 0.12959037293 —
2019 WASP-126 c — 39 2019 — — — —
WASP-18 c — 11 —
2019 LP 791-18 c 2.74432452 0.04739 0 96.5
TOI-263 b — 1.87 4.7869491 0.06555 0 87.19
PSR J2055+3829 b 6.78 1.676 9.15059 0.0814 0.066 88.54 —
0.00014 CWISEP J1935-1546 3.58 0.24614 19.98 0.137 0.168 88.795 —
HAT-P-70 b 0.02086 0.2614 4.65382 0.05186 0.194 88.92 —
HAT-P-69 b 0.0428 0.2432 — — 3.155 —
TOI-125 c 0.0299 0.000062 44926 26.3 0.63 58.6 —
2019 TOI-125 d — — 175.06 — 0.06 89.464
2019 TOI-125 b 50.5 0.053 —
2019 2I/Borisov
HD 13724 b — 18.57 0.1462 0.083 — —
2019 Kepler-1661 (AB) b 2019 — 5.2049 0.0664 0.083 — —
HD 38677 b — — 6.6732 0.0662 0.14 — —
2019 HD 11231 b — — 5.516 0.0651 0.07 — —
2019 HD 42936 b — — 6.584 0.0733 0.057 — —
2019 HD 38677 e — — 2.882 0.0422 0.07 — —
2019 HD 38677 c — — 0.719573 0.0166 — 82.1
2019 HD 38677 d 0.0176 0.1439 1.651144 0.02734 0.072 78.38
2019 HD 80653 b 1.463 1.02 3.739494 0.04666 0.024 85.68
TOI-564 b 0.667 1.171 0.04421 0.038 83.45 —
TOI-905 b 1.373 2.8641424
XO-7 b 0.709
2019 OGLE-2013-BLG-0911L b
EPIC 211939692.02 2019 10.08 — — 10.8 —
EPIC 211939692.01 — 0.232 39.553 — 0.06 —
USco 1621A b — 0.232 26.8549 — 0.16 —
2019 USco 1556A b 15 — — 2880 — — —
KMT-2019-BLG-0842 b 14 — — 3500 — — —
HIP 36985 b — 10.28 — — 3.31 — —
2019 WD J0914+1914 b — 8500 7 0.55 — —
Kepler-154 g — — — 0.07 — —
2019 GJ 40 b — 0.9145 1250 — 0.15 — —
OGLE-2016-BLG-1227 b 0.016 0.18066 5.746007 — 0.0385 0 88.57
HIP 41378 g — 0.79 — 3.4 —
beta Pic c 9.37 — 62.06 0.3227 0.06 — —
AB Dor C b 13 — 1238 2.72 0.248 97.86
TOI-677 b 1.236 1.179 — 0.58 — —
WISE 2150A b 34 — 11.2366 0.1038 0.435 87.63
HD 85628 A b 3.1 1.53 — 341 —
NGTS-8 b 0.93 1.09 2.82406 0.047 0 86.7
NGTS-9 b 2.9 1.07 2.4995 0.035 0.01 86.9
TOI-132 b 0.07183 0.306 4.43527 0.058 0.06 84.1 —
OGLE-2015-BLG-1771L b 0.98 — 2.1097008 0.026 0.087 84.63
Proxima Centauri 0.57 1.25 0.433 — 0.85 —
WASP-185 b 1.33 — 1894 1.48 0 —
WASP-184 b 9.38755 0.0904 0.24 86.8
5.1817 0.0627 0 86.9

—
1.083
0.0876 —
14.446 — —
0.16 —
tommy atkins
zill
alfonso
bez el-anza
oweisi
taymoor
dampara
hingurakgoda
karutha colomban
malwana amba
parrot mango
peterpasand
petti amba
rata amba
vellai colomban
willard
boribo muyini
dodo
mawazo
sindano
jin hwang
red jin hwang
tainong n 1
khaew sawei
nam dok mai
rad
brahm kai meu
okrong
haden
keitt
kent
tommy atkins
cao lanh cat chu
binh dinh elephant
hoa loc sand

2019 LSPM J2116+0234 b — 2019 — 0.019636 0.217 0.2 — —
2019 OGLE-2018-BLG-0532 b — — 41.516 0.099 0.2 — —
HIP 35173 b — — 15.144 0.063 — 2.15 —
HIP 54373 c — 7.76 — 0.0034 —
HIP 54373 b — 0.0267 0.0857 0.3 85.5
2019 OGLE-2018-BLG-0596 b — 0.0009 0.048 0.19 86.23
SDSS J1228+1040 b — 0.18601 3.58599 0.074 0.28 87.43
HR 858 b — 0.17299 5.97293 0.1027 — 7.2 —
HR 858 c — 0.19306 11.23 — 6.8 — —
HR 858 d — 0.57 — — —
KMT-2018-BLG-1990L b 4.9 — 1.13 0.0382 0
KMT-2018-BLG-1292 b 0.55 — — 3100 4.2 —
MOA-bin-29 b 0.229 1.136 3.3569866 — — —
NGTS-5 b 4.5 835 0.42 —
2019 OGLE-2018-BLG-0740L b 60 — — — 0.25 —
HD 221420 b — — 22482 9.75 0.085 89.89
Vir21 Sco b — — 10790 0.2068 0.105 88
HD 92987 b 0.595 0.91 34.5558 0.1293 0.24 —
TOI-216 c 0.082 0.767 17.085 1.487 0.15 —
TOI-216 b — — 649.918 0.143 0.14 —
HD 210193 b — — 25.2 0.041 0.11 —
HD 211970 b — — 3.2498 4.074 0.19 —
HD 39855 b — — 3090.9 0.439
HD 102843 b — — 120.878
HD 103949 b
WASP-175 b 2019 0.99 1.208 3.0652907 0.044 0 85.33
WASP-171 b 2019 1.084 0.988 3.8186244 0.0504 0 88.3
WASP-169 b 2019 0.561 1.304 5.6114118 0.0681 0 87.9
WASP-182 b 2019 0.148 0.85 3.3769848 0.0451 0 83.88
HD 206255 b — — 96.045 0.461 0.23 —
HD 21411 b — — 84.288 0.362 0.4 —
HD 64114 b — — 45.791 0.246 0.12 —
HD 8326 b — — 159 0.533 0.2 —
HD 24085 b — — 2.0455 0.034 0.22 —
HIP 71135 b — — 87.19 0.335 0.21 —
TOI-402 b 0.0227 0.1516 4.75642 0.05245 — 88.36 —
NGTS-6 b 2019 1.33 1.271 0.882058 0.016623018 0
KIC 10544976 (AB) b 2019 — — — 6136 6.56 0.29 —
HD 181234 b — — 7462.06 7.52 0.73 — —
HD 25015 b — 0.0901 — 6019 6.19 0.39 — —
K2-32 e — 4.34882 0.04951 —
HD 213885 c — — 24.16 — — — —
K2-294 b 2019 — 0.1472 4.78503 0.1344 — —
K2-293 b 2019 0.02778 0.2186 2.50387 0.056798 — 0 —
HD 213885 b 2019 1.19 0.15568 13.1225 0.036 — 85.5 —
Qatar-9 b 2019 0.736 1.009 1.008035 0.1 — 88.8 —
Qatar-10 b 2019 0.371 1.534 1.540731 0.02012 0 80.09
Qatar-8 b 2019 0.508 1.285 1.645321 0.0234 0 89.23 —
WASP-177 b 2019 0.017 1.58 3.71495 0.0286 0 85.87 —
TOI-270 d 2019 0.006 0.19 3.071722 0.0474 0 89.29 —
TOI-270 b 2019 0.299 0.11125 11.38014 0.0733 0.03957 — 84.14
WASP-181 b 2019 0.502 1.184 3.36008 0.0306 0 89.69 —
WASP-183 b 2019 1.47 4.5195064 0 88.65 —
4.1117771 0.04632 0.05427 — 88.38
— 85.37 —

concrezioni e storia naturale

se dici che sotto l'arco della mia spalla c'è un'intera stazione ferroviaria
un deposito con vuoti e pieni   si tratta allora forse
di tenersi nel buio di cercare quel punto tra le mani degli altri
dove una vena o un tendine non sono solo corpi
ma agglomerati in movimento
vicende umane   alberi e stagioni

perché cadere è una scelta e un apprendimento
che ha luogo solo nei corpi degli altri
il punto in cui qualcosa si annoda e annodandosi si apre
ai moti che uniscono i viventi sotto la volta dello spazio

questa forma del cadere e non un'altra
questo scivolamento collettivo e nudo ci sa dire
il rumore dell'inizio   la storia di coloro che
passati dall'arco del buio   hanno voluto essere toccati
al bordo del tappeto   alla fine del prato

tenere dunque   è   tenere insieme
questo il compito che ci è dato sopra al vuoto
la storia degli agglomerati che malgrado tutto   dici
malgrado tutto   sono vena e prato nudo
corpo unico e spazio   umani ed alberi in moto

Rihamuddin vive per strada e non ha niente se non il tempo
un tempo   di vita tra i quattro e i sei anni   cammina in cerca di cibo
illuminato come gli altri da un sole a cui non sta pensando

e attraversa insieme alla luce molte altre cose   una di queste scoppia
una scimmia fulminata dai tralicci dell'alta tensione
gli cade accanto dall'alto con un tonfo sordo

alcune persone escono stupite dai negozi   anche se accade spesso
Rihamuddin vede che la scimmia ha gli occhi chiusi ed è rannicchiata
a terra   ma una zampa si muove impercettibilmente e a scatti

sta guardando gli altri bambini accanto al minareto ed altri eventi ac-
cadono in un arco imprecisato   Rihamuddin ora ha una moglie   un'altra donna
abbandonata   e guida un tuk-tuk per le strade sterrate del centro

quando può si ferma e compra cibo al suo passato   beve un tè
pensa ai suoi figli   le scimmie camminano in alto lungo i tralicci
e la membrana di smog cambia colore a strati successivi   sulla città

la signora Marconi fa le pulizie in un condominio dove non abita
la mattina in metropolitana le accade di pensare a quanto segue

forse invece un giorno una parola potrebbe accadere fuori
da buio e luce   a liberare gli eventi dalle cause
tornando a casa   la gente più tardi   e si chiede
ma non è più una domanda   è una linea
un ammasso di galassie   un quasar che brilla lontano

la signora Marconi ha aperto la porta a vetri e sta in ginocchio
all'inizio delle scale scegliendo i detergenti che le servono

Cif
Ajax
Viakal
Lysoform
Quasar
Sole
Ariel
WC-Net

nota una porzione di sole che si estende lentamente
sul pavimento

«da quando lavoro ai macelli non sento più niente
sempre meno ogni giorno   mi sveglio alle 5 del mattino   in periferia
senza chiedere   ed esco in attesa che il giorno si estingua
ma oggi il vento muove rumorosamente ogni singola foglia
un insetto passa ronzando nella quiete assolata tutto cambia
ho paura di restare disoccupata ma qualcosa troverò

sulla piattaforma della stazione scelgo la porta socchiusa sul buio
da cui esce l’odore fresco e umido tipico di un cantiere   i fiori fuori
l’ombra opaca che si sposta   il bosco all’uscita dello stabilimento
benché tetro   rende sopportabile questo momento»

si vede vecchio allo specchio
ed un oggetto si spacca
il boccio si ammacca   cambia d'aspetto
si adatta

Samira è una ragazza di 15 anni
nel 2016 è stata rapita tenuta in cattività e *venduta ad almeno tre persone*
che l'hanno picchiata e aggredita sessualmente
prima di essere costretta a sposarsi e dare *alla luce un bambino*
suo marito è stato ucciso a causa dei bombardamenti *della coalizione*
e Samira è fuggita con il figlio nel campo di

alcune noci si riproducono cadendo dall'albero
dentro il mare e galleggiando
sulla superficie dell'acqua per alcuni mesi
raggiungono una nuova spiaggia da dove
poter germinare

Peter fuggì da solo
separato da sua zia e da sua sorella viveva nella boscaglia con altri sfollati
aveva dieci anni un gruppo armato lo ha reclutato
insegnandogli a caricare e sparare cucinare lavare i vestiti
e trasportare l'attrezzatura

nell'insediamento ogni bagno è condiviso *da più di 100 persone*
molti adulti hanno fatto ricorso all'uso dei *pannolini di notte*
per evitare di dover lasciare le tende e *fare la fila per*
andare al bagno al buio

strutture ovoidi pendono dalla cima di un albero
fuori campo

e poiché diceva «*mo mi piscio*» e voleva esser calato a tale effetto venne
calato *e poi disse* «*mo mi caco*» e venne tradotto alla latrina
per esser poi condotto al cospetto dei signori e interrogato dai signori
circa il suo nome rispose «mi chiamo fra Tommaso Campanella»

e visto che detto fra Tommaso Campanella se ne stava sempre in totale
silenzio *non faceva* il minimo movimento e sembrava che non sentisse
alcun dolore

per ora non hanno altra scelta che aspettare

se una libellula si librasse in questo libro

ci nascondiamo negli angoli delle stanze

spesso un decennio è sentito più che capito
dal colore delle immagini di una foto o un videoclip
che sembrano diversi dal presente   solo a distanza

che cosa siano gli anni 2000 è ancora difficile da dire
tanto meno i 10 o i 20   mentre possiamo cominciare a definire
gli anni 90 dal pastello opaco dei filmati VHS
e gli 80 sono ormai chiari a tutti   tra Terminator Thatcher
forme squadrate e tessuti cangianti

e se le pellicole   anche le più remote   possono permanere
la memoria invece evolve   è così che si torna
con la mente al cortile sul retro   che non parla
lo stenditoio di metallo arrugginito vibra leggermente
al vento   il suolo di cemento è arso   deserto
e le crepe da cui emergono erba e muschio sembrano
per un istante   nascite e messaggi

all'altezza di un insetto che ronza a mezz'aria
di un animale
o di un bambino che guarda
sono ombre i passaggi   gambe mute   uno stelo e un secchio
in un angolo   inutile tornare come quell'uomo senza volto a camminare
intorno a questo spazio   che si trova dicono alcuni
dietro una casa di periferia

tutto rimarrebbe indefinito anche da quella prospettiva
un pomeriggio caldo e nuvoloso muta nella mente ma non nell'ora
né nel colore che gli oggetti   obliqui   assumono per la rifrazione
di una luce deviata da cambiamenti   ostacoli   gravitazioni invisibili
e dalle forme diverse del tempo e del vuoto

tanto vale   talvolta   fare domande al giorno e agli anni
cercare di rendere la loro rotazione una cosa vissuta
adesso   anziché un'attesa o un intoppo della percezione

massa di gomma   massa di gomma
massa di gomma lasciata all'ingresso e mai più considerata
massa di gomma che unisci il corpo alla mente
la natura all'artefatto   massa di gomma non abbandonarci

mentre le mani gli occhi e i giorni
e ondeggia una palma in un vaso nella foto
dai colori opachi di un porto qualunque
mentre la gente litiga in televisione

presso un arco di mattoni in un parco di periferia
sotto il sole giallo di fine pomeriggio
un aggregato di materia aspetta senza dire niente
condensa una parte di tutto senza giudicare
né chiedere   la sua gioia è essere
massa   moto   vuoto   ed energia

«cercavamo dappertutto un sistema   un legame causale
tra loro e le foglie   un albero ricorda il vento del giorno prima?
sogna di fenomeni senza quantità   indistinti   inavvertiti
poteva andare peggio   poteva avere peso
schiacciare le cose sempre più ogni mattina
fino ad appiattire le scelte e a togliere il sole
come provenienza e messaggio senza oggetto
e noi esposti in mezzo a questa corrente ma distanti ormai
senza sapere come andare avanti quando si è
guardato ovunque»

e d'un tratto nella stanza c'è soltanto una persona
seppur con lampi rapidi   a tratti nella mente appaia ancora
l'altra   seduta sul bordo di una poltrona   come uno stupore
antico   per i colori della plastica e del vetro
scoperti su una spiaggia del passato

talvolta si vorrebbe   a sera   evitare la notte
dice un uomo di età incerta   con vestiti modesti
uscendo da un condominio
scendere a patti con il giorno già trascorso
come se potesse essere domani
ricomporre i vuoti e le bottiglie   accogliere gli sbagli preparati
scoprire che tra un ramo e l'altro non passa solo il vuoto

quanto durerà la gioia questa volta   quanto durerà
quest'onda   si chiede la signora Marconi
incontrandoci vicino all'ascensore

uno spostamento solletica la mia visione periferica

chi è?

sono la materia oscura
sono venuta a dirti che quella notte
sul ponte   avresti potuto fare diversamente
sarebbe stato forse meno onesto verso gli altri
ma certamente più autentico

le cose perse in questo universo
si ritrovano forse in un altro?

questo non posso dirti
in ogni caso non capiresti   strutture e relazioni
così diverse da quelle a cui sei troppo avvezzo

parli in modo un po' aulico
ma perché parli tra l'altro
e come fai per parlare?

anche a questo non c'è risposta che oggi
potresti capire

mi aggrappo alla memoria
ad esempio al ricordo dei nostri
corpi che in quel momento non potevano
avvicinarsi o al suo sguardo ambiguo
finché sono in vita questo almeno resterà

fai come vuoi   ma se ti piace la memoria
allora ricorda sempre che la tua vita
come individuo è solo una minima parte
della vita totale   a cui appartieni da sempre
e per sempre

amen   ma allora mi unirò
anche a te ad un certo punto
quando sarò finito come individuo?

come individuo sei sempre finito
e anche se per ora non lo senti
sempre preso come sei da te stesso
ti sto già attraversando

siamo una sola pelle   l'ignoto
spaventa solo chi vuole
il controllo

annotazione solo apparentemente banale
molti artefatti sono imitazioni
di cose naturali elicotteri per libellule
aerei per uccelli spade sifoni e recipienti

ma nessun corpo organico possiede pezzi intercambiabili
serpenti e mantidi cambiano la pelle come giacche
ma non possono rimetterla la frutta cade e non
si riattacca neanche ad altri rami
e nessun animale può separarsi da un'antenna o un arto
per poi rimontarlo altrimenti

neanche i sassi una volta divelti possono
sostituire parti della superficie da cui sono stati tolti
con la stessa esattezza dei tubi di un motore
o di un sistema idraulico o dei piedi
di un frigorifero delle zampe
di una lampada di eliche di ventole

(alcune ferite però possono rimarginarsi alcuni tentacoli ricostituirsi)

due insetti sovrapposti
come se fosse possibile scomporre il proprio corpo
in agglomerati di particelle   e mischiarlo
agli elementi architettonici   o ad un momento
di verde molto intenso

come se fosse possibile passare le transenne in aeroporto
mentre ti allontani tra i controlli sicurezza

La fabbrica trasformata

prima si cercava tra le rovine   oggi nelle facciate   prima si trattava di tracciare traiettorie oggi di percorrerle   prima di attraversare un oggetto nell'erba   oggi di attraversare l'erba con questo oggetto   prima di disegnare escrescenze   oggi di scavare buche   prima di scavare buche   oggi di produrre escrescenze   prima un recipiente conteneva il nostro pranzo   oggi ci si compra il pranzo in scatola   la storia è mutata ma muta

sotto l'umidità convessa dell'erba
sopra

e questo sole opaco dovevano vederlo anche loro   cercando   cercando di divenire parte del paesaggio verticale   cercando la linea del paesaggio verticale dietro lo spostamento verso l'interno dei cilindri   dietro il diaframma che li aveva portati dall'altra parte a cercare la linea del paesaggio verticale nel sole opaco che emana dalle colline intorno colline minerali rivestite da una pelle buia e lucida come i cilindri dentro cui ruotavano tutti insieme con le loro famiglie e le sere passate davanti alle stanze   prima di riprendere il gesto circolare e ritmico al posto delle macchine   queste macchine organiche rivestite da una pelle buia e lucida come le colline minerali su cui camminavano tutti insieme con le loro famiglie e le domeniche passate ad aspettare il sole opaco e il ritorno del paesaggio verticale dietro il diaframma   dietro la pulsazione del calore ad altezza delle macchine ad altezza delle colline all'altezza di questo sole chimico e del suo rumore che è oggi la storia di coloro che sono rimasti dall'altra parte del paesaggio   ad aspettare che le macchine tracciassero il gesto circolare   il gesto minerale   dentro i cilindri bui e brillanti come la pelle della storia   questa pelle liquida   questa pelle dell'acqua che non ruota più ormai non ruota più ma riflette immobile la base dei cilindri fino a sdoppiarli fino a spingerli nella terra nella pelle buia dello spazio   uno spazio minerale spinto sotto le macchine rivestito da edifici senza storia   da facciate più opache del sole che le illumina con la sua luce obliqua ogni sera ogni domenica prima di riprendere il suo gesto circolare al posto delle macchine dietro le colline intorno sventrate e appiattite da macchine costruite da altre macchine costruite al di là delle colline intorno dall'altra parte del paesaggio da altre storie   dalla stessa storia   la storia delle colline sventrate e appiattite per le famiglie e le sere e le domeniche passate ad aspettare il sole opaco e il ritorno di un paesaggio senza materia e senza macchine eppure verticale al di sopra della pelle dell'acqua che riflette immobile questi immobili senza storia e l'altro lato del paesaggio mentre il cielo filtra lo spazio con il suo sole opaco   con il suono sordo del suo sole opaco che si riflette sulla superficie buia e lucida degli uomini e delle macchine   dei cilindri e delle colline   delle sere della storia   questa storia che è come una pelle in cui vengono inseriti edifici spostamenti e forse   malgrado tutto   nuove storie e nuovi gesti circolari   strette orizzontali e minerali dietro le colline sventrate e appiattite sotto la pelle del paesaggio senza materia nel riflesso delle macchine sulla superficie dell'acqua   superficie che non ruota   la superficie liquida dell'attesa   la superficie degli edifici che pulsano nel calore del diaframma   nel calore del sole opaco e circolare che vediamo sulle facciate e che vedevano anche loro da un punto della loro storia minerale e orizzontale   loro e noi uniti sotto la pelle totale dello spazio fino alla distribuzione delle gocce durante la caduta nella buca

fino all'agglomerato delle gocce nel recipiente fuori dal recipiente fino alla distribuzione delle gocce fuori dal recipiente all'agglomerato delle gocce fuori dal recipiente alla caduta del recipiente al crollo delle pareti del recipiente fino al buco nella collina alla penetrazione del paesaggio per trovare o togliere secondo la distribuzione dei gesti nei secoli fino a scovare la buca toccare le pareti molli intorno alle pareti minerali fino alle membrane del recipiente nella fabbrica coprire la massa spingere l'energia ai lati come in un buco nero il buco nero della massa dei secoli e dello spazio le membrane opache della fabbrica le pareti porose penetrate dalla massa buia di una goccia smisurata o di un agglomerato di cadute

dietro la tenda

sta facendo la doccia più forze si concentrano questa mattina nello spazio la ascolto parlare e non è come altre volte ripensare gli agglomerati le traiettorie prima dell'orizzonte nel rumore dell'acqua che scorre adesso domani perché poi non ci sarà la ritroverò solo più tardi con i bambini sotto la luce gialla della cucina prima che il giorno finisca non ci sarà quando il flusso sarà denso e scuro in basso nel buco dei giorni e quanto accarezza adesso tra un'ora sarà ciò che spinge e controlla far scivolare linee e oggetti nella distesa dell'edificio e delle mattine un'origine per tutti i gesti sotto la pelle buia e lucida del buco dei giorni oltre la tenda da dove parlava quando il sole era ancora interno oltre la stanza dove l'ho vista quando il suo corpo era ancora inerte prima del risveglio questa fabbrica come il suo corpo questa mattina questa fabbrica come una risposta come un flusso denso come una nascita che come in natura non è scelta da chi nasce

Come se non fossero vis(su)ti

« voglio rendere omaggio ad un errore che ho commesso la porta della camera d'albergo si apre e la videocamera percorre un corridoio in soggettiva l'osservatore dall'altra parte dello schermo segue questa traiettoria ed entra in una stanza di un hotel moderno di media categoria con mobili di legno plastificato e un letto sul cui bordo si trovano due persone la videocamera rallenta quindi interrompe il proprio movimento in posizione frontale vengono fatte domande alle quali non possono inizialmente rispondere poi da alcuni sorrisi incerti escono parole confuse a bassa voce di fronte alla videocamera non sanno neanche come comportarsi da dove iniziare

né sanno fino in fondo se hanno scelto di trovarsi lì a parte per il denaro che è stato loro promesso sanno di poter produrre informazione digitale sotto forma di agglomerati di cui tuttavia non conoscono (né forse mai conosceranno) l'autenticità il loro corpo è comandato a metà e probabilmente questo processo è iniziato in tempi e spazi molto remoti

la pelle si distende solo esteriormente per l'interesse dell'osservatore 1 situato dietro la videocamera e dell'osservatore x situato dietro lo schermo questa informazione sarà venduta o forse condivisa gratuitamente con uno spot per finanziarla perverrà ad un numero imprecisato di persone che sapranno dove cercare e cambierà l'assetto psicosomatico la struttura vegetativa non so come spiegartelo forse voglio dire la capacità di empatia degli osservatori che riceveranno questa sequenza è pur sempre una questione di informazione che penetra la memoria che produce a sua volta informazione su un'area interna o esterna del corpo sull'osservatore 1 non so pronunciarmi se non per dire che la sua voce mentre fa domande e commenti indica qualcosa che si è perso per sempre

pur non potendo giudicare la natura di questa rappresentazione di uno stato di realtà o di una serie di eventi forse senza neanche accorgersene c'è un punto di non ritorno un movimento remoto di troppo e privo di scelta o di coscienza o una piega per quanto minima di una porzione di tessuto vista troppe volte mettila come vuoi da cui sarà molto più dura risollevarsi senza spostare a meno che non sia decretato come ultimo [*sic* probabilmente parte del messaggio è andata persa]

sul seguito della vicenda dopo il flusso di dati voglio dire una volta spento tutto possiamo solo formulare ipotesi forse l'osservatore 1 ha ripreso a percorrere il corridoio dopo averli pagati in contanti locali e dopo aver trasmesso queste informazioni saranno usciti da quella camera qualunque ma solo in via provvisoria si saranno salutati come da protocollo d'altronde non si erano probabilmente mai incontrati prima ognuno per la sua strada saranno andati a mangiare in un fast food credendo di aver scelto del tempo che si è dato a loro o forse volendo celebrare o chissà magari dimenticare un accaduto che si manifesterà in loro sotto altre forme rendendoli incapaci di cadere quando vorranno ma più esposti invece a una caduta costante e irreversibile ad una delle forme più pericolose della perdita quella in cui non si è coscienti di aver perso qualcosa e si crede di aver guadagnato quando invece per la natura stessa del tempo per lo meno rispetto alla nostra scala umana una volta rivelato un certo contenuto è impossibile riprenderselo non intendo come proprietà ma come forma da dare al buco che sta dentro a molti di noi e sicuramente dentro di loro sì come dicevo prima perso per sempre il tutto generato da chissà quali sequenze precedenti a cui neanche loro hanno accesso ormai forse gli osservatori x che avranno visto e non vissuto gli eventi potranno allontanarsi seppur in una dolorosa progressione da questa sequenza di dati organici rinfrescare lo schermo non basterà bisognerà credo uscire chiedere aiuto agli alberi e a chi conosce questo genere di informazione

non sarà necessario descrivere gli eventi nel dettaglio basteranno alcune coordinate instabili per orientarsi in uno spazio che resterà ciononostante invisibile e forse alcuni saranno salvati solo a quel momento si potrà parlare di libertà di democrazia e di paroloni simili adesso però devo lasciarti e riagganciare spero di risentirti ma non vederti mai di fronte a me come se fossi un'estensione di bisogni non avvertiti né riconosciuti va bene cercherò di aver presente quante più dimensioni possibili al momento del nostro incontro e le onde che si propagano in alcune di esse speriamo che »

[a quel punto il fruscio ha reso il resto della conversazione inudibile comunque sembrava quasi conclusa che ne pensate?]

concrezioni e storia naturale

l'*albedo (dal latino albedo* bianchezza) in botanica
è lo strato interno in genere di colore bianco
della buccia caratteristica degli agrumi

l'albedo (dal latino *albēdo* bianchezza) di una superficie
è la frazione di luce o di radiazione solare incidente
che è riflessa in tutte le direzioni

essa indica dunque il potere riflettente di una superficie
l'esatto valore della frazione dipende *per lo stesso* materiale
dalla lunghezza d'onda della radiazione *considerata*

se la parola albedo viene usata senza *ulteriori specifiche*
si intende riguardare la luce visibile

o

o

o

⊕

⊙

ricevo un colpo sul volto   e più tardi sento spari e grida in lontananza
provo paura   ho freddo   non so cosa fare

non sento più niente

o

le bolle di sapone fluttuano lentamente nell'aria
mentre tengo per mano mia madre nel parco
ne guardiamo la traiettoria   alcune   scendendo   urtano l'erba o
un arbusto   esplodendo senza rumore

diverse forme d'onda e luce producono eventi   sono deviate da oggetti
e non sono fatte per l'udito o la visione
i sensi scompongono segnali in dati per renderli materia
secondo criteri innati   ma con altri sensi questi movimenti
si comporterebbero in modi diversi

le radiazioni non richiedono sistemi di rilevamento
concepiti secondo un'intenzione   altri fenomeni invisibili
accadono solo in presenza di un osservatore
che può non avere organi di percezione   così ogni bacca lucida sospesa
sul suo arbusto non riflette tutto eppure il tutto
anche mentre nessuno passa
e un'area di sole inesistente si sofferma sulle piume di un uccello

come il cervo desidera *l'acqua alla fonte*
così una pianta di fragole scende da un terrazzo in cerca di terra
a cui potersi tenere   inviando una parte di sé ad esplorare il basso

il suono della voce della gente
si mischia al suono della voce delle gocce
e tornare in quella camera d'albergo a riprendersi
qualcosa lasciato sul tavolo   sotto la lampada verde
non è forse più necessario

la membrana esterna ed il guscio di un uovo
devono essere abbastanza porosi per far passare gas e nutrimento
e sufficientemente resistenti per proteggere la vita
almeno questa è l'interpretazione condivisa
di un legame causale

in altre aree invece il potere autorizza schiacciamenti
sparizioni e identità   azioni militari decisioni e spostamenti
di cui in fondo non conosce le ragioni

è che sotto   ci si dice   ricoperto dal raccordo periferico
bordato da alberi con le cime sfuocate
c'è un fiume fatto di vuoto e di tutto
anche se alle volte alzandosi dal letto
sembra che il soffitto diventi più basso
e le scale sospese nello specchio

o invece   perché un invece c'è sempre
una storia proteica dell'essere
i frutti aggregati ad esempio e cosa spinge

le drupe   i follicoli   gli acheni   a tenere insieme
l'uomo sumero di pietra verde a permanere
ininterrottamente   da quattromila anni   osservando gli eventi e la gente
senza bisogno di pupille   adesso dalla teca di un museo
anche mentre è il pensiero e non la presenza
che ci porta a lui

è tempo di entrare nella grande mensa
dove gli affamati cucinano insieme il proprio cibo offerto loro senza condizioni
e lo mangiano seduti a terra in una lunga fila da una parte all'altra dello spazio
poi dispongono piatti e vassoi   e li lavano dalla stessa posizione

è tempo di espandere la stanza in una distesa
e per la distesa di farsi erba mattino sole   estensione
di concetto e sostanza dentro al pensiero
dove ruotano cose quasi inesistenti   posate
da qualche parte   ma senza un luogo   e per questo spesso
neanche notate

PSR B1620-26c è un pianeta extrasolare *orbitante*
intorno alla pulsar PSR B1620-26 nell'*ammasso globulare M4*
è stato scoperto il 10 luglio 2003 sulla *base delle informazioni*
fornite dal telescopio spaziale Hubble
un sirfide sta sospeso in aria vicino al mio cappello
ci chiediamo cosa stia osservando ma una risposta certa
non è data ci siamo dimenticati l'acqua
puoi tornare dentro a comprare qualche bottiglia?
il pianeta dista circa 12400 anni luce dal Sistema Solare
ha una massa doppia di quella di Giove
e avrebbe circa 13 miliardi di anni

PSR B1620-26c dovrebbe essersi formato
prima che le stelle di Popolazione II dotate della sufficiente massa
necessaria alla formazione di un disco di materiale protostellare
orbitante intorno ad una stella genitrice
in cui fosse possibile la formazione di un pianeta
Mutteramo mammalbero Mutteramo mammalbero
Mutteramo mammalbero Mutteramo mammalbero
Mutteramo mammalbero Mutteramo mammalbero
Mutteramo mammalbero Mutteramo mammalbero
e suoni di piante e di uccelli al chiudere degli occhi ma soprattutto
una frequenza penetrante e ininterrotta che potremmo forse dire
il suono del sole
la presenza di tali elementi in corpi astronomici *antichissimi*
ha portato ad ipotizzare l'esistenza di una *Popolazione III*
di stelle di grande massa il cui collasso *avrebbe prodotto le reazioni*
nucleari necessarie alla fusione
devo portare la macchina in garage
devo cambiare il cellulare mi si è rotto lo schermo
devo ritelefonare al dottore per la prescrizione
devo rinnovare l'abbonamento in palestra
devo passare a ritirare gli abiti in lavanderia
in alternativa è possibile
che PSR B1620-26c fosse originariamente una stella
che ha poi perso per vari motivi parte della propria massa
spari grida e correre vicino alla polvere dietro le paratie
sotto una luce accecante
PSR B1620-26c è il primo pianeta *circumbinario*
scoperto tramite pulsar timing *le due stelle sono*
una stella di neutroni e una nana *bianca*
rendendolo così anche il primo oggetto
in orbita attorno a una nana bianca
dei nodi di luce si connettono dietro le palpebre
quando il sole filtra dalla pelle fuori dalle tende
del campo per rifugiati per una volta forse
alcuni di noi possono sentire solo queste
forme astratte date dai raggi nei bulbi oculari
e nel cervello anziché mani che strappano e conficcano
PSR B1620-26 è anche il primo pianeta *individuato all'interno*
di un ammasso globulare

del perdono della coagulazione
del sapone di cui si osservano i colori nella trasparenza
di alcune bolle che si spostano nell'aria

dei conflitti per la libertà dei gruppi dei soprusi e delle classi
degli abusi del potere che si annida in noi
anche quando crediamo di non averlo mai subito né cercato

di tutto questo senza parlare dicono
le orbite e gli ondeggiamenti di un cespuglio di more
mentre gli uccelli dicono altro ancora
e parlando fanno rumore

un sacchetto è rigonfio d'aria i cavi sono intrecciati
dove lo stelo si piega verso qualcosa
che possa dirsi luce

o in masse di tessuti e nervature nell'abbraccio che porta
la riconciliazione quando le cose dette o fatte
contano meno dell'aggregato senza nome che forse ascolta forse
permane anche all'interno della frutta
posata dentro un piatto vicino alla finestra

promemoria   dedicare una certa importanza alle piante acquatiche
ai loro intrecci e tra i tralicci della corrente
dal finestrino del treno   o raggruppate in vasche
parchi visti in sezione   dalla mente di un’elettricista
o di un giardiniere in una città di provincia
che chiedono aiuto all’interno di un armadio
mentre potrebbero affondare lentamente lungo il declivio
toccando la superficie liquida nel recipiente le opzioni
sono due   scendere e intrecciarsi
risalire la pianura
pensare in densità malgrado il vetro

le pompe devono vogliono normalmente funzionare sottobattente

la depressione nelle tubature di afflusso o aspirazione

non deve vuole superare 0.4 bar a pieno carico

e al livello dell'acqua più basso

la velocità di corrente nei condotti di aspirazione non deve vuole superare 2.0 m/s per una portata Qca

ogni pompa deve vuole essere munita di tubi di derivazione di emergenza che possano garantire a carico parziale almeno 1% della portata come acqua di raffreddamento

un tubo di controllo deve vuole essere collocato sul tubo di mandata prima della valvola di allarme in modo tale da permettere il controllo periodico della pompa a pieno carico

ogni pompa deve vuole avere un proprio condotto di afflusso o di aspirazione al quale nessun altro apparecchio può vuole essere raccordato

le caratteristiche delle pompe devono vogliono essere uniformi e includere i valori effettivi in base alla seguente rappresentazione (p + 0.4 bar 1.2 · Qca)

una medusa decide di essere portata dalla corrente
o si lascia portare e basta?
c’è una differenza tra queste due proposizioni?

può accadere che una medusa sia diffidente
di fronte all’ignoto dell’acqua
come noi prima di un orizzonte invisibile?

improvvisamente un traliccio visto dal treno in moto
appare come più denso di volume e storia
alcuni alberi hanno le cime fuori fuoco

una linea si dissolve   lascia spazio allo spazio
mentre l'esile fusto del luppolo sale lungo un traliccio
giorno dopo giorno   malgrado tutto

anche in quei punti sul bordo può accadere
una relazione tra gli ammassi di materia
tra i corpi
che riluce negli strati interni di oggetti

e concepisco il mattino mentre mi parli   come chiedere aiuto
il ramo dentro l'acqua che dica moti interi di persone   pianeti
stagioni   modi in cui la luce è resa obliqua dalle nubi
e traccia così un linguaggio sulle cose   qui come altrove
viventi ed oggetti uniti sotto la pelle infinita dello spazio

o   vuoto   o pieno   buco nero o orifizio
o come un pianeta   una bolla   un sasso   un'arancia
o un'orbita   una lettera   un anello   una giostra
una polla circolare dove l'acqua vibra
per i moti impercettibili del suolo
un'indecisione   un'alternativa   un'esclamazione
un modo di tornare   in movimento circolare

a questo odore delle stagioni che persiste

Lettera all'inosservabile

cari amici   la giostra gira qui da molto tempo   se di tempo si può sempre parlare visto che lo spazio è una stanza senza coordinate   uno di voi ha detto una volta   ricordo che se nulla ha senso allora tutto ha senso   e il vuoto esiste per noi in una serie di strati di profondità   quindi come qualcosa che possa dirsi materia

è così che il volo imprevedibile di una falena vicino ad un lampione mi è apparso d'un tratto a sera   dopo cena   come una scrittura nel buio   le sue traiettorie generavano un significato che era di un ordine diverso rispetto a queste stesse parole

similmente il moto di un giunco nell'acqua   e le sue vibrazioni più intense quando su di esso si posa una libellula   non spiegano niente   non annunciano niente   eppure sostengono questo linguaggio   e ritmano il pensiero che dal mio corpo arriverà forse alle vostre menti oppure resterà nella sabbia come un suono   e andrà bene anche così

cari amici   mi dispiace di avervi lasciato partire sotto la luce gialla del pomeriggio lungo i vigneti declinanti verso la fine dell'estate   per tornare dentro casa ad aspettare la pioggia che batterà sul tetto e sui vetri   ogni goccia un concetto   o un evento

in effetti   amici   vorrei in fondo che mi perdonaste senza chiedere niente   e che accettaste i miei sbagli senza riserve   vorrei ricevere il vostro bene anche se il vento può modificare l'orientamento delle cose ed esporne lati mai visti prima

vorrei che non aveste più rimpianti   che i vostri occhi   anche se affaticati dal calore del corpo e dagli anni   potessero percepire ogni molecola   ogni particella che   orbitando compone gli oggetti dati alla nostra esperienza senza una ragione unica né una necessità al di là del fatto che ci sono e che ci siamo

ma soprattutto   amici   vorrei che vi teneste gli uni negli altri   senza lasciare fuori nessuno   e che foste casa l'uno per l'altra   e pioggia che scende lungo la curva   anche della sua parte oscura e inosservabile   dove le linee parallele possono ancora convergere   se continuiamo a cercare e a cercarci   fosse anche in nome di una conoscenza senza comprensione

non riesco a rinunciare alla possibilità di saperci   noi tutti   ancora acqua e sole   anzi liquido e luce   paesaggio e orizzonte che si crea dentro ogni onda   o goccia   o ramo spostato dall'aria ed esposto così ad una nuova inclinazione   non posso non sperare di ritrovarvi tra queste foto sparse di fronte a me   scattate l'estate in cui ci ritroveremo tutti insieme   a casa amici la pace la libertà fanno paura lo abbiamo imparato a caro prezzo e queste parole sembrano persino banali agli occhi di alcuni ma forse non per coloro che hanno scelto di tornare su quel cesto pieno di melograni sassi forme del pensiero

si tratta in fondo lo sapete di camminare lentamente sulla coltre di alghe nere attaccate alle rocce e di girarsi verso le cime degli alberi che gonfiandosi appaiono fuori fuoco sottraendosi alle facili regole della visione a distanza si tratta forse in questa lettera che ho scelto di mandarvi della possibilità che esista un modo per salvarci

cari amici mi mancate anche se non so chi voi siate e spero che tornerete nell'attesa se di attesa si può parlare visto che il tempo è una stanza senza coordinate non rinuncio a pensarvi come linee di nubi sulla curva di un orizzonte visto dall'alto e cerchi di luce attorno a un campo gravitazionale o pietre raccolte su una spiaggia inondata dai raggi obliqui di fine pomeriggio

AUTHOR'S NOTE AND ACKNOWLEDGEMENTS

This work, like many of my projects, explores the possibility of poetic language as a contribution to contemporary conceptual art and thought in general. More than ever I have attempted here to transmute into language phenomena, organisms, concepts, feelings and events that do not originally belong to the linguistic sphere, for cognitive, emotional, and political reasons. The typographical devices, such as, for example, the superposition or inversion of words, have no particular relationship to visual or concrete poetry, but have rather emerged from the run of the text itself and from the 'multidimensional' experience of meaning that the text tries to unfold. While differentiating itself completely from the formalism of socalled 'uncreative writing,' several sections of this text were elaborated from specific sources, in particular legal documents, articles, websites, and books of philosophy, botany, and astrophysics, sometimes quoted exactly, sometimes lightly rewritten.
In the book the exact quotations are distinguished from my 'original' texts (but what in the end is an original text?) by three-dimensional typesetting (curved and/or slanted), for reasons I will leave to readers to discover.

The sources from which I quoted (there are obviously many more on which I drew indirectly) are, barring lapses of memory, the following:

- Giovanni da Palestrina, *Sicut cervus*, Rome, 1608;
- Luigi Firpo, *Il supplizio di Tommaso Campanella: narrazioni, documenti, verbali delle torture*, Rome: Salerno Editrice, 1985;
- Swiss fire protection systems handbook *Sprinkler-Anlage* (thanks to Remo Dell'Anno for this document);
- Michael Perryman, *The Exoplanet Handbook*, Cambridge University Press, 2018;

- *The Extrasolar Planets Encyclopedia* (exoplanets.eu);
- Jack J. Lissauer & Imke de Pater, *Fundamental Planetary Science*, Cambridge University Press, 2019;
- M.S. Swaminathan & L.S. Kochar, *Major Flowering Trees of Tropical Gardens*, Cambridge University Press, 2019;
- Reports by Médecins Sans Frontières and Save the Children;
- Documents of the United Nations High Commissioner for Refugees;
- Wikipedia and YouTube.

The poem "passed from one hand to another at the market stall" ("passato da una mano all'altra al banco del mercato") was born from a travel story told to me by Joëlle Tuerlinckx.

Previous versions of several texts in this book were written and published following commissions from the Munich Staatsballet (for *Portrait Wayne McGregor*, 2018), from the Biennale Gherdeina VI in Ortisei, curated by Adam Budak in 2018, and from the project "*Be*Have – Public Art Experience" in Luxembourg, curated by Delcroix & Pinsky and Hubertus von Amelunxen in 2016.

Following these and other invitations, previous versions of several texts in *And agglomerations, of Trees Or* were published in the following books, anthologies, and magazines:

- "il buio del sonno corrisponde forse al nero dello spazio" appeared in *DEARS*, year 1, n. 1, Zurich, 2020 (in Italian and with a different English translation by myself and Laila Dell'Anno);
- A previous version of "if you say that beneath the curve of my shoulder" – "se dici che sotto l'arco della mia spalla" appeared in Bayerische Staatsoper, *Portrait Wayne McGregor* (Italian, English and German, translations by Andreas Burckhardt and Laila Dell'Anno respectively);
- Different versions of "anche se la nebbia forma una membrana sulla distesa", "«dopo una notte difficile»", "le linee curve della cima", "dentro l'inizio del bosco", and "e concepisco il mattino mentre mi parli" appeared in A. Budak (ed.), *Writing the Mountains*, Catalogue of the Biennale Gherdeina VI, 2018 (Italian, English, German, and Ladin, translations by Andreas Burckhardt, Laila Dell'Anno, and Milva Mussner respectively);
- A different version of *The Converted Plant* appeared, in French, in A. De Francesco, *Three Poetic Engines – Trois engins poétiques*, Paris: MIX & Luxembourg: Le Fonds Belval, 2016.

And Agglomerations, of Trees or was supported by a 2021 "Writing Space" grant from the Swiss Foundation for Culture "Pro Helvetia".

I wish to thank: Marco Mazzi for believing in this project from the outset and producing it so wonderfully; Judith Balso for her insightful preface and for the essential support she has always given to my poetry; Ilaria Bombelli, Simona Spadoni and Matteo Gualandris at Mousse Publishing for having so closely and generously followed the realisation of this book; Max Norman for his masterful and creative translation of such a complex text; my mother, Paola Cerrai, for her falcon-like proofreading; as well as the artists, writers, curators, editors, translators, cultural organizers and financial backers who have made this project possible.

Alessandro De Francesco

some lines are not relevant for a tree
a rock   a jellyfish
but deep down we all need
to be something instead of nothing

so every event is maybe only an aggregate
born of substances in large part unknown
and not of a series of choices

alcune linee non sono rilevanti per un albero
una pietra   una medusa
ma in fondo abbiamo tutti bisogno
di essere qualcosa anziché niente

così ogni evento è forse solo un aggregato
che nasce da sostanze in larga parte sconosciute
piuttosto che da una serie di scelte

Alessandro De Francesco
and agglomerations, of trees or
e agglomerati, degli alberi o

Published and distributed by
Mousse Publishing
Contrappunto s.r.l.
via Pier Candido Decembrio 28,
20137, Milan–Italy

Available through:

Mousse Publishing, Milan
moussemagazine.it

DAP | Distributed Art Publishers, New York
artbook.com

Les presses du réel, Dijon
lespressesdureel.com

Antenne Books, London
antennebooks.com

Idea Books, Amsterdam
ideabooks.nl

Design
Simona Spadoni, Mousse

Printing
Intergrafica Verona, Italy

This publishing project has been
produced by Marco Mazzi.

ISBN 978-88-6749-530-6
18 € / 20 $